PASSIONATE PILGRIMAGES

PASSIONATE PILGRIMAGES

From Chopin to Coward

Elizabeth Sharland

WELCOME RAIN PUBLISHERS
NEW YORK

ISBN 13: 978-1-56649-051-1
ISBN 10: 1-56649-051-0

Dedicated to the memory of Sheridan Morley

Acknowledgments

Jacques Alonso, the Noël Coward Society, John Gander,
Sandy Paul, Gerald and Colman Jones, Paul Webb

Contents

Preface

Part of the legacy the personalities in this book left us was their enthusiasm for travel, often because of their work, but often in search of creative ideas. All these people were connected with and wrote for the theatre.

During their lives, however, they went on passionate pilgrimages—sometimes to resettle and live in a different country, sometimes just to acquire a second home.

Their work revolved around these travels, especially on the part of Somerset Maugham, because of the numerous short stories written during and derived from his travels.

PASSIONATE PILGRIMAGES

Introduction

My first job was working with the Old Vic Company in London when Richard Burton and Claire Bloom were playing the leads. Laurence Olivier and John Gielgud were acting in the West End and it was the golden age of British theatre.

I have had several books published on the theatre and speak regularly on the topic. My passion for music and drama has been the primary source of joy in my life, so I have made it another passion of mine to travel across Europe, and to a few other exotic locales, to visit the places where famous musicians, writers and artists lived, loved and worked.

Romantic love, passionate love, theatre people's love for the theatre. Poets, playwrights and actors all experience the anguish of having to choose between their love for the theatre and their love in their private lives. What do actors, writers and composers do when they are not working, or their muse deserts them, or their private life falls apart?

It is interesting to discover some of the haunts of legendary actors, writers and composers who found solace in finding new places in which to live and possibly to work.

To rely on the creative impulse constantly may sound self-indulgent, or at least to involve a tremendous amount of anguish and torment.

For instance, Simon Callow, the actor who appeared in *Four Weddings and a Funeral* and many other stage and film productions, writes in his book about being an actor that he nearly went mad when he was out of work. At one point he says he was in a state of continuous turmoil, and if he hadn't started to write he might have gone insane. One of his most impressive works was a biography of the famous English actor, Charles Laughton.

The urge to write and make pilgrimages to places glorified by the heroes and hero-ines of our imagination is a deep one, beginning I believe, in one's childhood. What images would be conjured up by the town of Stratford-on-Avon if Shakespeare hadn't been born there? What is Athens, other than the home of the great playwrights of antiquity—Aeschylus, Sophocles, Euripides and Aristophanes, the writers Plato, Aristotle and the philosophers? Travelers can go to places where characters, possibly entirely mythical, once lived, such as Mycenae, Troy and, closer to home, Baker Street. Practical difficulties are no obstacle. The conquest of Palestine by the Turks led to the First Crusade, which established a European kingdom there, and in spite of changes of governments over the intervening centuries, pilgrimages still continue.

In the following chapters we will visit some of the homes of the celebrated, includ-ing the Somerset Maugham Villa Mauresque, in the south of France. Maugham should be an inspiration to all struggling playwrights, writing plays for ten years before he had his first produced. After his struggles he gained fame as a writer of short stories and at one time had four plays running simultaneously in London's West End. His home for many years and where he died was the Villa Mauresque on Cap Ferrat, and behind the gates of the villa is one of the most beautiful places on the French Riviera.

Somerset Maugham wrote the novel *The Razor's Edge,* which is a classic tale about one man's voyage to search for and find out for himself the meaning of life. When I first read the novel it had a profound impact on me and I was fascinated by the idea of retracing his journey in the book, to more deeply understand the character's moti-vations. So I suppose my passionate pilgrimages are partly to assuage or to discover the feelings or emotions that these artists' lives evoke. Obviously they had passions of their own, and they had their heroes, their ambitions, their goals. One wonders what moti-vated Maugham to write about the people he met during his world travels. Who were his heroes? And who were the heroes of Keats and Byron?

I was born in Tasmania, which is the little island off the south coast of Australia, below Melbourne. My brother and I grew up listening to grim accounts of my grand-father's explorations in the undiscovered mountains of Tasmania. They were horren-dous—of battling against fierce, unexplored bush in tremendous storms, with tents and food being swept away in howling gales and no relief in sight for weeks. They made me realize just how primitive the conditions and difficult those ordeals must have been. Perhaps descendants of explorers, I thought, might inherit the genes of their ancestors, and the energy or motivation is born in you. I certainly thought that having hiked through many mountain ranges, later opened up by my father, stood me in good stead when exploring more civilized parts of the world. At least my grandfather had a mountain named after him in Tasmania, which I suppose must have justified his effort. Sharland's Peak lies southwest of Devonport in the north of the island.

There must have been a spiritual need to try to explore the island, similar to the need some people have to trek to the Himalayas and for others, to have reached the top of Mount Everest—first.

The choices people make, when they have the opportunity to choose, reflect their personalities as well as their values. Some people choose to be limited by their occupations or their way of making money and spend their lives in the same place or country where they pursue this limited ambition. Others consider themselves citizens of the world; they consider nothing human as alien to them, and therefore feel that they are aliens nowhere.

They travel and explore. While there is little nowadays to explore in the sense of being first to see some part of the earth, there is the opportunity to live in other parts of the world other than one's native place.

Portrait of George Sand

Chapter One

George Sand and Chopin at Château de Nohant

The man that hath no music in himself,
Nor is not moved with concord of sweet sounds,
Is fit for treasons, stratagems, and spoils:
The motions of his spirit are dull as night,
And his affections dark as Erebus:
Let no such man be trusted.
　　　—Shakespeare

George Sand was one of the most remarkable women writers in France during the nineteenth century. She was not only a famous novelist, essayist, political figure and playwright, but also the lover of the Polish composer, Frederic Chopin. She was born in Paris in 1805 and died at her château at Nohant in 1872.

There have been several films made about Sand and her life at Nohant, where she lived for many years with Chopin. Several years ago the BBC made a series on her life called *Notorious Woman*, starring Rosemary Harris. The introduction shows Rosemary standing at the window of Sand's bedroom looking out on the garden at Nohant. The film follows her life, her friends, her lovers and the people who made her one of France's most famous women.

I was taken to a concert of Chopin's music when I was twelve years old. The pianist was not Rubenstein or Horowitz but could have been as far as I was concerned. The next day our music teacher at school took our class to see the film *Song to Remember,* which tells the life story of Chopin. It is a colorful film, with actors in sumptuous costumes and scenes in which Chopin is playing in the great concert halls of Europe.

I had been a reluctant piano student at school since I was eight years old, rarely practicing, but these two events changed the next ten years of my life. Walking home after the film I was overwhelmed by the music, determined to learn and play the music which I had just heard. The Polonaise, the waltzes, the mazurkas—I was so passionate about it all. This immortal music totally consumed me. It became an obsession, to learn it all, which seemed to please and surprise my piano teacher immensely. I knew it would take hours, days, months to do this, so my after-school hours and weekends were totally occupied. A twelve-year-old with raging hormones can achieve a great deal. I was determined to play the Military Polonaise, without mistakes, at the year-end school concert.

Entrance to Nohant

The film became a classic. Though some of the dialogue could be 'sent up' today, the essence is still there, similar to *The Red Shoes* or *The Seventh Veil,* a spirit which inspired hundreds of students to study and practice to become concert pianists or ballerinas. Even now teenagers, full of energy, drive and ambition are awakened artistically by these special films.

My passion continued and a scholarship to study at the Guildhall School of Music and Drama in London followed. For ten years I studied to become a concert pianist but it wasn't to be because of a number of things. Finances were one; more important, I knew I didn't have that extra touch of genius that one must have to rise to the top in the professional music world.

While I was at the Guildhall, I had to take a second course, so I chose the theatre, since I had fallen in love with Chopin's lover, the French novelist and playwright, Aurore Dudevant, known to the world as George Sand! (She was played by Merle Oberon in *Song to Remember.*) I read all the biographies about her I could find, and my group at the Guildhall discussed the relationship between her and Chopin. Did she actually sleep with him, or was she a mother/nurse figure to him? Many biographers claim there was no sexual relationship at all, but how then did he attract such attention from the society women in Paris? Sand was regarded as a wicked woman, because she had slept around in the literary world in Paris—so why not with Chopin? His music is so full of romance, beauty, anguish and sadness, it is hard to believe that Chopin and Sand weren't in love. During this time, I tried to commune with both of their spirits; I thought that if I talked to them enough that they would appear. (Shows you what eight hours of daily practice at the piano will do to you!) Now, years later, I decided to visit the château at Nohant and see for myself where they worked, lived, entertained and most of all to see it while it remained unchanged.

Visiting Nohant was one of my first passionate pilgrimages. I felt as if I had been there before. Even though it is called a château, the building is the size of a small manor house and it belonged to Sand during those years Chopin lived there with her.

The house and garden at Nohant are still the same as they were when she lived there. I took some recordings of music that I knew Chopin had composed there. There are long covered paths in the garden, where he must have walked while composing those melodies in his head before writing them down, so I sat on a bench there and listened to them. Fortunately there were no other visitors that day.

Chopin's piano at Nohant

Chopin's piano and all the furniture is original down to the place settings at the dining room table, with the place names of whom she invited for dinner, including Flaubert, Turgenev and the painter Delacroix, who painted both Sand's and Chopin's portraits during their lifetimes.

Sand had four plays running simultaneously in Paris and her novels flew off the shelves in the bookshops beginning around 1830 onward. She was celebrated and well-known before she met Chopin but of course became immortal as his lover and nurse when he suffered from tuberculosis. Today, her books are hardly read, and her plays remain unproduced. Yet, because of her relationship with Chopin, her fame lives on.

Sand's maiden name was Aurore Dupin. Her father was of aristocratic lineage as his father was the son of the Comte de Saxe and a cousin of Louis XVI. Her mother who was living in Paris fell on hard times and was forced to take her daughter to stay with Aurore's paternal grandmother who lived at Nohant. She began to educate Aurore and teach her the aristocratic ways of the upper class. Aurore loved the country life; she loved horses and rode everywhere. She was taught languages and excelled in her studies. When her mother came to claim her, she didn't want to return to Paris but chose to remain with her grandmother at Nohant, who left the estate to Aurore when she died.

Aurore married Baron Casimir Dudevant in 1822, and they had two children, but it was a sad marriage as her husband was not of the same class. Even though he was a Baron, which made her a Baroness, they were very unhappy. He drank and was unfaithful. As the story goes, he physically abused her on their wedding night. On the night she gave birth to their son, he was sleeping with one of the servants at the château and was informed of the birth later that night. Finally, his behavior was so intolerable to her she knew that one of them would have to leave. As Casimir had become the manager of all the property, the farming, the stock and all things relating to the estate, Aurore decided that she would have to leave, to preserve her sanity and to escape from his abusive behavior and drunkenness.

She went to Paris with little money, and was determined to work and meet new people. She decided to write articles for two magazines in Paris, as she was aware of the political problems of the day, as well as the artistic scene and the emerging talents of other writers. Life was very difficult for her and she had to rely on strangers to help her. At that time in Paris, many of the writers were using drugs and they were as fashionable as marijuana was in the 1960s. There, she became somewhat notorious as a man-killer. She met some young writers and fell in love with several of them. She shared a flat with one of them, Jules Sandeau, with whom she wrote a book. She decided that being a woman was a handicap when sending manuscripts to editors, so she adopted a pen name, taking part of Jules's name, Sand, and adopted the first name

George. She wore men's clothes, because they were cheaper and warmer and she could also go to the theatre and stand with men in the stalls, whereas the ladies had to buy a seat which was far more expensive. She began smoking cigars and socialized mainly with men. When she split with Jules Sandeau she moved in with Alfred de Musset who was a well-known poet, and he introduced her to opium.

Every six months she would return home to Nohant and try to sort out the paperwork and finances that Casimir had been attending to. His drunkenness had become worse, and her half-brother, whom she had relied upon to keep an eye on her husband had also become a drunkard. Finally, she got rid of them both and decided to spend more time at Nohant. She was missed back in Paris and Alfred de Musset came to find her.

After she returned to Paris she and de Musset went to Venice, where de Musset became desperately ill and almost died before George found a doctor who saved his life. Sand was so grateful that she had an affair with the doctor, which caused a split from de Musset on their return to Paris.

When she met Chopin she was living in Nohant most of the year and she invited him to stay with her. He was already quite weak although no one knew how ill he would become. She thought he needed warmth and the sun, so she arranged for them to go to the island of Majorca for a holiday. When they got there they found the place cold, wet and wintry. They had difficulty finding a place to stay and finally found accommodation at an old monastery, a few miles out of Palma. Their rooms were part of the convent, had stone walls and floors, and were icy cold with hardly any heat. They were very uncomfortable without the support of servants or any kind of medicine. A piano was shipped to Chopin so he could work, but the weather and conditions were so appalling that the couple were forced to leave and return to Nohant, Chopin's health being even worse than before.

Sand continued her writing and Chopin his composing. They had visitors from Paris whom she entertained by having a small theatre built next to the dining room on the ground floor, where they presented her plays. The theatre is still there today, and the stage is still set for one of her plays. Chopin sometimes played to accompany the action when there was a pause in the dialogue. She also had a puppet theatre made for her son, Maurice, and she took time to make the puppets, their costumes and the sets, and wrote the scripts as well. The costumes and the puppets are still in good condition,

Dining room, Nohant

as is the little theatre. It was their way of entertaining themselves and their guests, much as is television today. Her plays were tried out there, before they went on to be produced in Paris. It is incredible to think of how she managed to raise a family, run the house, take care of Chopin and write over one hundred novels. She found a method that suited her. She would stay up all night and write, then sleep in the mornings when the household was up. Since her novels were so popular, she explained that the publishers were so impatient to get the new one that she never rewrote.

Finally her daughter, Solange, announced that she wanted to marry the sculptor, Clesinger, who was poor and unpopular and had a bad reputation in Paris. Sand was totally opposed to it, and told Solange she wouldn't allow her to marry such an unsuccessful sculptor. Solange went to Chopin for sympathy, asking him to intervene on her behalf with her mother, which he did. Sand was irate and asked both Chopin and Solange to leave. This caused a final split with Chopin, whom she saw only briefly at a concert months afterward. Solange did marry Clesinger, in the little chapel in the village of Nohant. It is ironic that the life-size statue of a grieving woman over the grave of Chopin, in Père Lachaise cemetery in Paris, was done by Clesinger. It is still there.

After Chopin's death, Sand lived out her life in the country at Nohant. She became known as the grand lady of the region, an earth-mother figure, who wrote books about nature in the region of Berry. She was also a great hostess, and many famous figures came to pay homage to her. Flaubert was a frequent house guest, as were Turgenev, Delacroix, Liszt and Countess Marie d'Agoult. She died an agonizing death in 1876 at the age of seventy-two three weeks after suffering a bowel obstruction. Doctors felt it was too dangerous to operate and could do nothing, except try to ease the pain. She is buried in the garden at Nohant, close to the little chapel where Solange was married. Her son is buried there also.

When you visit Nohant today, you will see the artwork that her son Maurice painted on the front foyer and around the circular staircase that leads up to the first floor. He also had a large studio leading off this floor, which is the only part of the house that is closed to the public. You can see the studio where she worked, which is next to the room where Chopin composed. All the original furniture is still there. The view from her bedroom window shows the garden and the little lodge where she would go for solitude and meditation, no doubt when Chopin was composing at the piano.

When I walked through the house there was a sudden burst of fresh air through the open French windows and it seemed as if the draft stirred up the smells of the old house. The house was still fragrant from the scent of the wood floors, the French furniture polish, the wood paneling, and the fresh flowers. Standing in the little theatre, I examined the tiny puppets just three inches away from me, displayed in a glass case, puppets that Sand had handmade, sewing all the costumes as well as making their china faces and full wigs, from what looked like real hair. The small stage in the theatre had pieces of furniture from the last set she had used for one of her plays. You felt as if the characters would just walk in and start acting.

I relished the silence, although it must have been a bustling household, with not only her children and servants living in the house, but the comings and goings of any large house which has a farm attached. I tried to imagine in that silence, what it must have been like and how much I would have given to have been there then even for a day.

The emotion which stirred within me was of profound sadness. The glorious music that Chopin had composed here had not brought him personal happiness—only suffering as he became ill and Sand turned against him. The reality of just how hard all the artists in this book worked somehow is immediately apparent when you see their homes. But it was at Nohant, most of all, where I felt that deep sadness and hoped that at one time in their lives that Chopin and Sand had been happy.

The French government owns the house and grounds, taking care of the upkeep of both, otherwise the château would have become derelict due to neglect and the rising damp. Each year in July there is a festival of music at Nohant, where famous pianists come to play at concerts in a large barn adjacent to the château. Reservations are essential as it is booked up well in advance. There are daily tours of the house throughout the week.

Somerset Maugham

Chapter Two

Somerset Maugham and the Villa Mauresque on the Cote D'Azur

Like most people, I discovered Somerset Maugham's short stories and novels before the plays. During my time in London studying the piano and theatre, I came across his short story called "Alien Corn," about a young man aspiring to become a concert pianist. Obviously, I was fascinated by the subject, as this was my ambition as well. In the story, the parents of the young man invite a famous concert pianist to come to listen to him play, probably for a fee, with the understanding that this celebrated musician will tell them if the son really has the genius to become a professional pianist. Alas, the young man is informed that, while he has a great feeling for the music, he doesn't have that extra brilliance needed. Later that day, the young man takes one of his father's guns and shoots himself, leaving a note to the effect that if he cannot spend his life as a concert pianist, he has decided he no longer wants to live. The story was very upsetting to me at the time, and still is. It remains one of the iconic stories of our time about the passion needed to attain excellence in any field.

Maugham is a hero to many of us in the theatre, as his passion kept him going, sustaining him during the ten years it took for the first of his plays to be produced in 1930. After these early struggles he eventually came to have four plays running simultaneously in London's West End, and he, of course, also gained great fame for his stories and novels. Movies based on his work are still being made in this new century. I have devoured all his work, and visiting his home on the Riviera in France was a trip I decided to make as soon as I could afford it.

Maugham was born in Paris in 1874 in the British embassy, to which his father was legal consultant. For his first nine years, Maugham spoke only French, and for the rest of his life was as much at home in France as in England, although his writings and the biographies about him mention few French friends or acquaintances. It is tempting to compare his mastery of English and indeed his style to that of Joseph Conrad, whose native language was Polish. Maugham also was fairly fluent in German, but less so in Spanish and Italian, and it is interesting that in his memoir *Summing Up* he declared that there was no particular merit in learning any foreign language except French, although when working as a British spy in Russia during the First World War, he was hindered by his limited capacity in the Russian language. (In *Summing Up* he also writes that he had been asked on occasion whether he would be willing to live his life over again. "On the whole," he wrote, "it has been a pretty good life, perhaps better than that of most people, but I should see no point in repeating it.")

His mother, to whom he was very close, died when he was nine years old, and his father two years later. He was then taken care of by a clergyman and his wife in Whitstable in Kent. He was an unhappy, shy child with a stammer that made him the butt of his schoolmates' taunts. Nevertheless, he became a medical student and qualified as a doctor, though he never practiced. However, he believed that the experience was useful to him as a writer, having given him both knowledge of the lives of the poor and training in the scientific method and logical thinking.

He was never poor himself, since he inherited a modest income, which enabled him to mix with people much richer than himself; he was quite sociable and indeed fun-loving as a young man, but always conscious of the importance of money as a means to independence and the procurement of the more enjoyable things of life. Still, his early adult life was marked by struggle. He wanted to be a writer, but he had difficulties interesting publishers and agents in his plays and novels. It was not until he was in his early thirties that he began to achieve fame and fortune with the production of his play, *Lady Frederic*. From that point on, his career was in the ascendant. Maugham entrusted his earnings to a good friend, Bertram Alanson, who invested them wisely, and in a few years, he had become a millionaire.

He was lionized both in England and the United States. He used his wealth to become an adventurous traveler, and he used his travel experiences as material for his books. He was particularly interested in the Far East and took some hazardous voyages there, and once nearly drowned. He also contracted malaria, which plagued him intermittently and almost killed him. However, his keen observation of British people living in the Far East and on the Pacific islands was the basis of many of his stories and plays, notably the story "Rain." He continued to travel to the Far East into old age, but his success as a writer about the East diminished. His last trip resulted in nothing at all. It may be that his increasing preoccupation with himself, his ideas, his philosophy, and his health progressively lessened his curiosity about others' lives and experiences and writing about them no longer seemed worthwhile.

Like many then and now, he loved the Mediterranean coast. He was drawn back to France from London and in 1926 bought the Villa Mauresque. He immediately employed two architects for renovations, which took more than a year, but he finally moved in to what would be his home for the rest of his life, except for during the war years, when it was occupied by Germans and vandalized. He had it cleaned up after the war, and his furniture and pictures, which had been given over to friends for safe-keeping, were returned.

He was seldom alone there; for a man who was reputed to be shy and diffident, it is remarkable that he had so many guests at what became a continual house party. His friends and guests included rich and titled people as well as those celebrated for artistic and literary achievement: Noël Coward, Hugh Walpole, Pablo Picasso and others. He had married Syrie Wellcome, daughter of the orphanage founder Thomas Barnardo in London in 1917, with whom he had a daughter, Liza. However after a very difficult marriage they divorced in 1927. He went to live in the south of France with a male companion, Gerald Haxton. When Haxton died, he invited Alan Searle to live with him, to whom Maugham willed the Villa Mauresque. As soon as he had inherited it, Searle sold the Villa Mauresque and the surrounding grounds to a developer. However the Villa stands as a place of pilgrimage to those whose lives were affected in one way or another by his work.

I finally made my journey to see Villa Mauresque in 1983. Impressive wrought-iron gates between the stone pillars, one of which has Maugham's insignia inscribed on it, open into a flower-bordered driveway that curves its way up to the villa, which is hidden from the road. On your right you pass by the tree-lined tennis court which Maugham had built for his house guests.

The villa itself, appearing enormous from the driveway, is not that large inside. The architecture is Moorish and the inner courtyard is gracious and airy. Walking through the main rooms on the ground floor, you come out onto a large patio and swimming pool. The main bedrooms are on the first floor with a corridor looking out onto the courtyard. On the third floor was Maugham's study where he had blocked out the view from the window so he could work without distraction. Walls throughout the house once displayed an impressive art collection, which was on view at the Theatre Museum in Covent Garden before it closed.

Author outside the Villa Mauresque

Just down the road in this exquisitely beautiful part of the world is the famous Hotel du Cap where Maugham was a frequent visitor. It is worth a visit alone to have a drink on the terrace, or to take the cable car, situated at the bottom of the garden, to the Beach Club below. There is a path winding around the pine trees and rocks at the water's edge which provides a delightful way to soak up the atmosphere and spirit of Cap St. Jean Ferrat. I felt exhilarated by the whole area, the sweeping view of the sea from the Villa and the hotel. The thought intrigued me, that Maugham entertained most of the great writers of his day in this hotel's bar! The F. Scott Fitzgeralds, Cole Porter, Noël Coward, the Murphys, and all of them had been equally enchanted with the atmosphere, the cuisine, the beautiful gardens and the water glittering below. Their signed photos can still be seen in the bar today.

Hotel du Cap

In fairness, to fully experience the creation of Maugham's art, one would really have to travel everywhere he did, but as with all great literature, reading about travel is the closest thing to traveling. Maugham wrote about the romance of traveling, and his stories evoke the excitement of a world then far away, where people lived strange lives, sophisticated or simple; these characters are unforgettable. His cynicism and knowledge of human nature sometimes leave you shocked and depressed, but he never fails to move you. The tales of the British shipboard companions or, reading between the lines, his own experiences, are fascinating. He was an explorer, not only of geographic areas, but of human emotion.

Chapter Three

Ivor Novello in London

Songs that help and support people and families in time of war often live on for generations. As a young child, you might have heard your mother or grandmother singing or humming a song which meant a great deal to her, but hardly anything to you.

I remember my mother singing Irving Berlin's song "Always," and Dad used to whistle "I'd like a nice cup of tea in the morning" when he was shaving in the small pantry off our kitchen, where the water ran hotter than in the other taps for some reason. My grandmother used to sing "Pack up your troubles in your old kit bag, and smile, smile, smile," which brings us back to the songs that were written during the First World War. They awaken nostalgia and passionate feelings of hope from that time, yet they were written to distract us from the horror and carnage in the trenches, where thousands upon thousands of our soldiers died. "Troop songs," they were called, and since they were sung to cheer up the families back home, it didn't matter if the words became blurred.

My grandmother was a Royalist, who loved the Royal family back in the early 1900s. Every time she heard a military band playing "Land of Hope and Glory," or "Soldiers of the Queen," tears would come into her eyes as if she remembered each and every one who had fallen in the war. She lost a son and a brother in that war. She used to ask me to sit with her, when she was old and too tired to walk down the stairs to have a cup of tea with the rest of us. So I would sit with her and she would tell me stories of the Grenadier Guards and of the other guard regiments she knew about.

Her affection and dedication to the Empire were typical of many people of that generation. Their loyalty to the Crown and the country was quite exceptional. She instilled in me the excitement of far-away places, of travel and distant lands, where she had been in her youth. Her stories were exhilarating, especially on those down days when the daily schedule of school, homework and chores was especially boring or difficult. In this way, she widened my world.

But the world she knew then has now disappeared, as well as the British Empire and a certain pre-television way of life. She was graceful, elegant and well-mannered. She was caring of other people and a great Bridge player. She taught me many things besides those songs: how to identify real pearls, how to know real jewelry, how to dress, when to wear short or long evening gloves—in fact, everything you would expect a grandmother to know. I used to read to her. She liked Georgette Heyer's novels and books about antiques. She loved shipboard life in those days and would travel abroad on her own, playing bridge and meeting people. One of her favorite performers was Ivor Novello, whose war song, "Keep the Home Fires Burning," is still played occasionally. Years after she died, I went to London to find the flat where he composed that song. I finally managed to locate it.

After decades of almost being forgotten, with the advent of Cameron MacIntosh and Andrew Lloyd-Webber's new musicals, year after year, it is surprising to know that in 2006 the name of the well-known and popular Strand Theatre in London was changed and renamed the Ivor Novello Theatre. I thought how pleased my grandmother would have been with that news. Thinking about her, the nostalgia and love for her made me want to find his flat.

A Visit to Ivor Novello's Flat and a Stroll Down The Strand

Ivor Novello was the first superstar. He was only twenty-one when he composed "Keep the Home Fires Burning." At twenty-six he was a silent movie star. In his thirties he was Britain's biggest male box-office draw, and he had a string of successful plays in the West End, in which he was both star and playwright. In his forties he returned to his original love—music—and dominated British musical theatre with a string of smash hits at Drury Lane. He maintained this phenomenal workload through the 1930s and 1940s. When he died at age fifty-eight in 1951, he was starring in his musical *King's Rhapsody* and had another hit, *Gay's the Word,* which he had written for Cicely Courtneidge, playing in the West End as well.

He seemed to epitomize the glamour, the success and the sheer enjoyment that theatre—both musical and not—represented. He had the added advantage that—

Ivor Novello

although he was every bit as glamorous as Noël Coward—he was, in relation to Coward, relatively unknown to younger generations; so I had the added excitement of feeling that I was discovering an extraordinary secret when I came across his work. Ivor—as everyone used to call him—devoted his life to the theatre, over and above his love of music, though he combined the two wherever he could. That is why his musicals were such a success; he put all of his remarkable talent, energy and enthusiasm into each production. The title of one of his last songs, a tribute to the Edwardian stars he had watched as a boy, could as easily have applied to him. It was called "Vitality."

This love of theatre, which I shared, had been expressed in his choice of home. He lived not just in or near the theatre district, but above a theatre (The Strand) in the

Aldwych, next door to the Waldorf Hotel, a few yards from the Aldwych Theatre (which hosted the farces written by Ben Travers, a wartime colleague of Ivor's in the Royal Naval Air Service) and opposite the famous Gaiety Theatre, which was, sadly, pulled down in the 1950s and turned into offices.

Ivor died nearly sixty years ago, and the world that he represented—the music and the romance of the Edwardian era, the magic of the silent movies, the glamour of the inter-war years with their jazz-age fashion, smart restaurants, beautiful clothes and spectacular musicals, the heroic defiance of German bombs during the Second World War, and his defiant production of lavish all-star shows in the otherwise austere post-war years—seemed to have all disappeared, along with the Gaiety Theatre, the Saville Theatre (where his last show, *Gay's the Word,* had been produced), and the society restaurants like Romano's and the Café de Paris.

What was left? A blue plaque, one of the commemorative signs placed on the houses of the famous by English Heritage, has been placed by the door to Ivor's flat. Every time one waits for a red London bus in the Aldwych (usually in the inevitable London rain), the plaque reminds passersby that "Ivor Novello, Actor-Manager and Composer," once lived there. Purely by chance I discovered that though it was now a suite of offices, it was, suitably, the London base of a leading theatrical impresario, Duncan Weldon, whose beautifully produced, star-studded plays at the Theatre Royal, Haymarket and other such grand venues would have earned Ivor's approval.

I took my courage in my hands and phoned his office, explaining that I was a theatre historian with a special interest in Ivor Novello, and could I please have a look round what had been his home for so many years? The answer was immediate—"Yes!" On the appointed day I rang the bell outside the door to the flat, which was wooden, old, and would doubtless have been recognized by Ivor. I was lucky—since my visit it has been removed and replaced with a dull, bland, modern piece of glass and chrome. As the door buzzed open I entered the little hallway to find myself face to face with the famously small and unreliable (though slightly modernized since Ivor's day) lift. As I ascended in this tiny wooden contraption, which on many occasions had threatened to trap numerous celebrities between the floors, I remembered reading Noël Coward's description in his autobiography *Present Indicative.*

"The Flat sat, and still sits, on the very top of the Strand Theatre, and, in order to reach it, a perilous ascent was made in this small, self-worked lift. Ivor's guests crushed themselves timorously together in this frightening little box, someone pulled a rope, there was a sharp grinding noise, a scream from some less hardy member of the party, then, swaying and rattling, the box ascended. Upon reaching the top, it would hit the roof with a crash and, more often than not, creak all the way down again. The big

Plaque outside Novello's London home

room of the flat had a raised dais running across one end. Upon this were sometimes two grand pianos, at other times none; sometimes a gramophone, and nearly always Viola Tree, an actress and close friend. The high spots of the parties were reached in this room. Charades were performed, people did stunts. Olga Lynn sang, and Fay Compton immediately did an imitation of Olga Lynn singing."

When I reached Mr. Weldon's offices I was given free run of the place and, though all signs of the original furnishings had gone, the shape of the rooms, even down to the dais that Coward had referred to, was still there, so the whole place seemed strangely familiar. I would not have imposed, but a secretary asked if I would like to go onto the roof. Thus, I even managed to see where Ivor, who loved to sunbathe and who, like his friend Noël Coward, had bought a home in Jamaica to avoid the worst of the English winter, had lapped up the sun when in London.

This love of the sun had taken Ivor abroad whenever he had the chance, and his first film, *L'Appel du Sang,* directed by Louis Mercanton, was set in Italy. He had been given the part in 1919, just after the First World War. During the war he had earned fame and fortune at the age of twenty-one when, in 1914, he wrote "Keep The Home Fires Burning." Already a published composer whose work had been performed at the Albert Hall, Ivor decided to write a patriotic song to preempt his mother, who had been threatening to compose one herself. Had she been able to write one before her son, the family reputation would never have recovered.

Ivor already had the melody in his head when he invited a young American poetess, Lena Guilbert Ford, to write the lyrics. It was in the flat above the Aldwych, as Ivor played the tune on the piano when inspiration struck. It had been a particularly cold day, and as Ivor and Lena sat together, the maid came in and laid some fresh logs in the fireplace. "That's it!" he cried, "Keep the Home Fires Burning!" He immediately wrote down the words of the chorus, and Lena wrote the verses. Sadly, she was not able to benefit from their joint effort as she and her baby were killed during a Zeppelin raid on London.

Ivor tried for an air career, but after two plane crashes, his commanding officer decided that he was causing more damage than the Luftwaffe, so he was given a desk job in Whitehall. This was highly convenient for him, not only because he was a short walk from his flat in the Aldwych, but he was within walking distance of the West End, where his songs were appearing in a number of revues and musical shows.

It was, therefore, as a composer that he was famous in 1919, when Louis Mercanton approached a casting agency, looking for a handsome, dark-haired young man to play the role of a hot-blooded Latin lover in his new film. It did not take Mercanton long to spot the soon-to-be-famous Novello profile. "That's the man!" he exclaimed, and, when told that the boy was a composer, not an actor, he refused to be put off.

Ivor's background and professional life were in music, but the theatre was the great love of his life, and he jumped at the chance to be an actor. True, his performances were on the silver screen rather than the stage, but silent movies required highly dramatic acting (and makeup), so this was an excellent introduction to an acting career; besides which, how many young men without any drama school training are offered the lead role in a glamorous French movie as a first job?

Ivor's later career as actor/manager/composer, with a string of hit musicals to his name, saw him cast as an Englishman (albeit in lavish foreign surroundings), a Viennese composer and a Ruritanian King. Attempts to play Italians were abandoned after his disastrous appearance in Noël Coward's play, *Sirocco*. Since this was not one of Coward's best plays, it had taken a great deal to persuade Novello (who knew his limitations) to accept the part of a sultry young Italian. The first-night audience took an immediate dislike to the play in general, and hisses were heard from the gallery, along with increasingly loud and frequent ad-libs to the text. When Ivor's character sulkily claimed that he was about to go to his mother, a ribald response from the gods suggested what he might do when he got there!

The play went down in West End history as a synonym for disaster. Noël Coward's mother, whose deafness had been the prime cause for her son's adoption of his famously clipped tones, turned to her son and asked nervously: "Is it a failure, dear?" Coward by name, courageous by nature, he was determined to confront the audience's dislike of the performance. To be fair, not everybody was hostile, and the physical blows that were swapped between his supporters and his detractors enlivened the proceedings in the stalls. All this culminated in the curtain call, when Ivor and his leading lady, Frances Doble, led the cast in bows that met with a storm of abuse from the enraged patrons in the gallery. The stage manager, almost as deaf as Mrs. Coward, took the catcalls and boos for signs of enthusiasm and kept ringing the curtain up for yet another bow. It was the custom, in those days, for the author not only to take a first-night curtain call, but to make a speech of thanks, to cast and audience, from the stage. Before he could say anything, Frances Doble, by then in a state of hysterics, stepped forward to give her curtain speech, too shocked to say anything other than the speech that she had prepared earlier in anticipation of the usual Noël Coward first-night success. "Ladies and gentlemen," she stuttered, to renewed tirades of abuse, "this is the happiest night of my life." The play soon closed, and Ivor and Noël's friendship survived the most traumatic theatrical failure of either man's career.

Coward followed Kipling's famous exhortation in the poem "If," by treating disaster and triumph in the same way—he got on a ship and sailed away. Whether it was to celebrate a success or flee from a failure, to recuperate from illness, to overcome one of the nervous breakdowns that afflicted him as a young man, or simply to recharge his batteries, Coward loved to get on a ship and steam off into the sunset.

Ivor joined him in buying a house in Jamaica, which in the 1940s was a fashionable place to go for the sunshine. Lord Beaverbrook, the newspaper magnate, was a neighbor and friend on the island. Ivor sailed a lot less than Noël, though he had enjoyed his fair share of transatlantic trips in the days when sailing was the only practical way to travel to and from New York. On one occasion he had been due to sail home from the States, only to find that the stray dog that he had adopted was missing. Refusing his friends' request to leave the wretched dog to its own devices, he postponed his departure until, after a day or two's delay, the dog turned up. Ivor's famous generosity and kindness worked in his favor on this occasion, for the ship that he had been due to sail on was involved in an accident that led to its sinking a little way out of New York and the loss of hundreds of lives.

He did not let this incident put him off cruising, however, and ocean liners were to be a feature of several of his spectacular 1930s musicals. In a radio interview in later life, he described how his parents' home in Cardiff had been the center of musical and theatrical life in the city, and he had grown up surrounded by beautifully dressed stars, giving him a taste for glamour that had stayed with him all his life. Ocean liners were then (and still are, despite the social changes of the intervening sixty years) seen as the epitome of glamour, so it is appropriate that one featured strongly in the first of his Drury Lane shows, the aptly named *Glamorous Night,* in 1935. This has as its hero a young English television inventor, who travels to a remote country named Krasnia in search of fame and fortune. Ivor's musicals were heavily influenced by those of Lehar and other Edwardian composers whose work Ivor had seen as a young man, and, despite the inclusion of some very topical themes—after all, television was in its infancy in 1935—his musicals are very much in the Viennese operetta tradition. Having arrived in Krasnia, Ivor saves a famous opera singer, played by the American star Mary Ellis (whose own career began at the New York Metropolitan Opera during the First World War) from assassination. The reason for the attempt on her life is that Mary is not just an opera star, she is the King of Krasnia's mistress as well!

One of the themes of Ivor's shows was the importance of duty and doing the right social and moral thing, so in order to save her royal lover from further embarrassment, Mary goes on a cruise—and so does Ivor, who has fallen for her charms. As you would expect, both of a cruise ship and of a Novello musical, the liner is the last word in luxury and romance, highlighted by a stunningly beautiful stowaway, the black American cabaret star Elizabeth Welch. Miss Welch sings a shanty but is otherwise unengaged, as the ship swiftly proceeds to sink, providing an astonished first-night audience with a spectacular special effect, using all the technical resources of the vast Drury Lane stage.

Once shipwrecked, Ivor and Mary land safely ashore and discover a gypsy encampment, where they are made welcome. Gypsies are something of a running theme through Novello's career. In one of his early silent movie successes, *The Bohemian Girl*, in which he starred opposite the young Gladys Cooper, he plays a Polish nobleman who is similarly sheltered, in his hour of need, by a troop of gypsies, improbably led by that epitome of upper-class elderly English gents, C. Aubrey Smith! This being a Novello production, the gypsies in *Glamorous Night* are an unusually glamorous group, and when Ivor and Mary decide to have a gypsy wedding, their newfound friends find them stunning wedding clothes, and they themselves appear at the ceremony in national costume covered in brocade and dripping with semi-precious stones!

Glamorous Night received the rare accolade of a visit by King George V and Queen Mary. The King's tastes in music were philistine, to say the least. When asked for the name of his favorite opera, he replied that it was *La Bohème*—"Because it's the shortest"—and when asked the name of his favorite tune, he said, without a second's delay, "God Save the King." Despite the show's royal stamp of approval, the owners of Drury Lane had hedged their bets by booking in a pantomime for the winter, so *Glamorous Nights* had a surprisingly short run. The following year Ivor pulled off another success, with *Careless Rapture,* a wide-ranging show that involved Chinese brigands, oriental temples and a full-scale earthquake on stage. In 1937, he had been asked to insert another scene at sea, and he duly obliged. Having portrayed and then sunk an ocean liner in *Glamorous Nights,* he felt he had to do something a little different this time round, so he added a transformation scene in which the liner was made into a battleship!

At the end of each night's performance at the Theatre Royal, he would be mobbed by legions of fans, mostly female, outside the stage door. These days many stars are not prepared to meet their public, or to do a bare minimum of autograph signing before being whisked away by bodyguards and limousines. In the 1930s there was still a tradition that stars owed a duty to their public, and Novello was famous throughout theatreland not just for his good nature and ready, matinee-idol smile, but for his attention to his fans. Every night, once he had greeted the celebrities (British luminaries like Noël Coward and Gladys Cooper, or visiting Americans like Joan Crawford and Douglas Fairbanks, Jr.) who crowded into his dressing room, he would appear at the stage door and sign as many autographs as necessary, his profile lit to full advantage by the stage door light, before being driven the few hundred yards home to the Aldwych in his Rolls Royce with monogrammed doors.

The last of his shows to be presented at Drury Lane was *The Dancing Years,* which opened in 1939. The Lane was taken over, for the duration of the war, by the armed forces' entertainment agency, with its acronym ENSA—affectionately known to the troops as "Every Night Something Awful." *The Dancing Years* spent the war years on tour and at the Adelphi Theatre in The Strand. It was while he was starring in *The Dancing Years* at the Adelphi that Ivor served a month's prison sentence in Wormwood Scrubs, a notorious north London jail. The cause of this extraordinary sentence was his beloved Rolls Royce, which transported him back to the Flat during the week, and down to the country house, Redroofs, on weekends. Strict petrol rationing made this impossible, but a female fan, who claimed to work in a senior capacity at a firm based in Maidenhead near Redroofs appeared to have found a legal way round this problem.

Unfortunately, it turned out that her obsession with Ivor had got the better of her, for she was employed as a clerk, with no authority to arrange deals between her firm and Ivor. When this came to light Ivor was charged with conspiring to break the law. The government wanted a rich and famous scapegoat to make an example of, and although the normal punishment would have been a fine (as Noël Coward found when he broke the currency laws), Ivor was sentenced to jail.

This mean-spirited and spiteful gesture backfired terribly, for the sentence was so clearly unjust that the public reaction was very much in Novello's favor. When he returned to the stage of the Adelphi after his month's absence, there was a storm of applause and cheering from the audience, who confirmed his place as the King of the West End musical.

Although his reputation survived, his health was broken by the experience and so, according to many friends, was his spirit. Having spent his life in music and the theatre, a beautiful and talented man surrounded by the most attractive and gifted people in London, creating superb plays, films and musicals for several decades, the shock of being thrown into prison was appalling. He survived and wrote two more spectacular musicals, *Perchance to Dream* (1945) and *King's Rhapsody* (1949), but his health, which had never been very strong and had not been helped by his habit of chain-smoking cigarettes throughout his adult life, was permanently weakened, and he died while still in his professional prime.

His very last show was *Gay's the Word*, written for his old friend, Cicely Courtneidge. She had been a musical star and comedienne since the First World War, thanks partly to the fact that her father, Robert Courtneidge, was a leading impresario of the late Victorian and Edwardian eras, and thanks partly to her stage partnership with her husband, Jack Hulbert.

Cecily's career had been in decline, and Ivor, whose generosity was well known, promised to write the music for a show with which to revive her fortunes. His usual lyricist was the immensely talented Christopher Hassall, but for this show he teamed up with Alan Melville, whose witty lyrics were perfectly suited to this lighthearted piece. The show's protagonist is a retired star of the Gaiety Theatre, the bastion of Edwardian musicals that stood exactly opposite Ivor's flat, on the other side of the Aldwych. It was a glorious building, outside whose stage-door top-hatted Edwardian men-about-town used to wait for the Gaiety girls before escorting them into their carriages and off to supper at one of the innumerable society restaurants. Sadly, the theatre has since been pulled down for office development. All that is left is a simple plaque, which reminds us of another London theatre that has been lost forever.

Gay's the Word's central character is called Gay Daventry (hence the title), who sings a song about herself, called "Gaiety Glad." Cicely Courtneidge's best-known song from this show, however, was a number called "Vitality," which she adopted as her theme song for the rest of her career. In "Vitality" she recalls the great names of the Edwardian stage, like those of Phyllis and Zena Dare, whose careers had been given a second lease on life through Ivor's shows. The song is a celebration of British musical talent that is both affectionately nostalgic and defiantly defensive, as in the line: "Give me Gracie Fields instead of any crooner." The fact that it was Ivor's last show made it all the more poignant, and many people can still remember the first night, when a clearly ill but still sun-tanned and elegant Ivor appeared in a box at the Saville Theatre to watch Cicely Courtneidge's triumph. At the curtain call the audience spontaneously turned to him and applauded, but in a characteristic gesture he waved his arm at the stage and told them their cheers should be for the star, not the composer.

In one of the countless press interviews that he gave in the course of his nearly forty years at the top, Ivor was asked how he wanted to die. His reply was very specific— that it should be on stage, at the end of a curtain call speech after a tremendous success starring in one of his own musicals, with the applause still ringing in his ears. Apart from the ghastly injustice and humiliation of a month in prison, his life was one glittering success after another, and he was granted a death that only missed this ideal scenario by a few hours.

On March 5, 1951, he had appeared as usual in *King's Rhapsody*, one of his best musicals, in which he played the Crown Prince, and subsequently King, of a Ruritanian country. He had been determined to fight back against the postwar fashion for American blockbusters by writing a defiantly old-fashioned English musical, with kings and queens, twenty-one gun salutes, ballrooms and jewels, and with trademark Ivor Novello music, full of show-stopping songs and memorable melodies.

His leading lady was an unknown he had discovered, employed and promoted— Vanessa Lee. He had even changed her name, from her real one, Ruby Moule. He had thought the name Vanessa suited her character, and having worked in the West End with the young Vivien Leigh (née Hartley), he decided that the surname—spelt differently, of course—would bring her luck. Among the other women in the show were several of his old favorites, the Dare sisters (Zena playing his mother, Phyllis playing his mistress!) and Olive Gilbert, who, with Muriel Barron, had been the first to sing

Ivor's most popular tune, "We'll Gather Lilacs," in *Perchance to Dream*. Olive, a stout lady with a superb contralto voice, was one of Ivor's closest friends and supervised the staff at his Aldwych flat, as well as generally ensuring that everything in his off-stage life was comfortable and properly arranged. She had the little flat beneath his and was summoned upstairs in the early hours of the morning on the 6th of March.

Ivor had returned home after the show, in the company of his producer Tom Arnold, a highly talented man who produced a whole range of entertainments, from Ivor's musicals to ice shows and pantomimes. After the inevitable bottle of champagne, he had left, though he was concerned at the twinges of pain that Ivor felt in his chest. After midnight the pains returned, and Ivor's friend, Bobbie Andrews, who lived with him, called Olive upstairs. A doctor was called, but he could do nothing, and as he, Olive and Bobbie stood, helpless, Ivor passed gently away from a heart attack. True, he had not died exactly as he would have wished, but he had had another hugely successful evening in the lead of his own show, had celebrated with his old friend and business partner, and died in his beloved Aldwych flat with two of the people he was closest to at his side.

Just as the Gaiety Theatre and the way of life that it represented have been reduced to a small plaque on a dreary modern wall, so ended the life of one of the most extraordinarily talented men of the London stage and the British cinema, who kept the British musical theatre alive over twenty years. But though it may mean little to tourists waiting for transport to St. Paul's Cathedral or office workers going home after a long day's work, to anyone with any knowledge of or interest in theatre and music, that plaque, and the flat it refers to, is shorthand for the glamour, spectacle and style of Ivor Novello.

The London theatre and hotels that Novello and Coward frequented are still open and now there are two theatres named after them. But the first one they both loved was the Savoy. This theatre was conceived by and built for Richard D'Oyly Carte with the express purpose of staging the Gilbert and Sullivan operettas which he had produced with such success for many years. It opened in 1881 and was the first theatre in London to be lit by electricity. It was built on the Embankment in the grounds of the former Savoy Palace Hotel, the predecessor of the present Savoy Hotel, and the entrance was originally on the Embankment. For the first fifteen years almost nothing other than the Gilbert and Sullivan operas were played there. Subsequently there were a few seasons of revivals. With the exception of a few other musicals, notably Noël Coward's *Sail Away* and a musical version of his *Blithe Spirit,* it has been, with the exception of its early days, the home of legitimate theatre.

The best-known patron was probably Winston Churchill who usually occupied the Royal Box. Many other famous names are associated with the theatre: Harley Granville-Barker, better known now as a playwright, produced in the years before the First World War two seasons of Shakespeare's plays which were extremely well received. Noël Coward had several of his plays done there, including *The Young Idea,* in which he also played. Laurence Olivier starred in *Journey's End* in 1929. Robert Morley, starring in *The Man Who Came to Dinner,* brought the play the fame that it so richly deserved. Margaret Lockwood had a two-year run in the 1950s in *The Spider's Web.* One could go on and on; the Savoy remains one of the favorite theatres for Londoners.

The Strand

Almost too extravagant in both its architecture and its interior decoration, the Strand Theatre was built in 1905, and has been operating nonstop since then in spite of having been bombed in both World Wars; on neither occasion were the performances more than briefly interrupted. Celebrated plays produced there for the first time include *A Funny Thing Happened on the Way to the Forum,* which ran for two years, and *No Sex Please, We're British,* which ran for eleven. *Cabaret* ran for a year, and Tom Stoppard's *The Real Thing* also had its first production there. *Arsenic and Old Lace* ran for a couple of years during the Second World War. Charles Laughton played there in *Bachelor Father* in 1927, before he started his film career. The theatre has now been renamed the Novello Theatre.

Novello Theatre, London

Giacomo Puccini

Chapter Four

Puccini in Lake Lago, Italy

My pilgrimage to see Puccini's house in Italy was years after I had first heard his music and read several biographies about him. I had been to visit Verdi's house just outside Bussetto and felt as if he was still in the next room because the house has been kept just as he left it. His furnishings are still there, as well as the wonderful garden and little grotto, to which he no doubt retreated in the midsummer heat of July and August. However, my pilgrimage to Puccini's house was largely motivated by Franco Zeffirelli's film of the making of Zeffirelli's opera production of *Tosca*. (He had already made the definitive version of Verdi's *La Traviata*, which interprets the emotion of the music as well as anything onstage.) I wanted to see where someone as great as Puccini had worked, entertained and played, and organized duck shooting expeditions, which he loved enormously. It is curious to learn that someone who could write the aria "Vissi d'arte" could then presumably put on hunting clothes, collect his guns and go out on a duck shoot.

There were many other distractions as well. He had many mistresses, for example, thus causing his wife extreme anguish, but nevertheless he could describe and capture the essence of despair and romantic love. His music is glorious and I wanted to discover the world at Lake Lago he so much loved.

His music is loved by millions, and also by the singers who have interpreted it, from Maria Callas to Placido Domingo. They have their own passionate following, and anyone who listens to Maria Callas singing a Puccini aria will never forget it. Numerous books and even a play, *The Lisbon Traviata,* have been dependent on the emotional brilliance of Callas's singing. To go to see where the music was written was another passionate pilgrimage for me.

The House at Torre Del Lago

In 1894 Puccini discovered the house at Torre del Lago, a little inland, near the shore of a lake. He bought the villa, and while he was living there he composed *La Bohème,* which had its premiere in 1896, and, subsequently *Tosca,* which premiered in 1900 in Rome. This villa is worth a pilgrimage. Imagine an undistinguished town, a nondescript road leading to the edge of a lake, where the villa stands. As we were driving through the town, which seemed deserted, I began doubting the wisdom of looking for it. We had turned off the main motorway, the express route to the south, miles back. The landscape all was flat and uninteresting—we found ourselves in a very ordinary Italian suburb with overhead tram lines, lots of transport trucks and bicycles everywhere. We turned left along the lake road and there was the villa standing back slightly from the main road—a plain stucco house overlooking the lake. Fortunately, it was open.

The front door leads directly into a small entrance area, then straight into the parlor. Puccini's upright piano stood against the left wall. A small table at the end of the keyboard held a lamp over it. It was here he did his composing, next to the piano or on the piano stool itself, simple enough but somehow impressive. This was his home until 1921 when he had a villa built at Viareggio, and then moved there. The move was necessitated by the construction of a peat factory, the fumes and noise of which drove Puccini to relocate. However, he never sold the villa at Torre del Lago; he returned occasionally to pursue his favorite recreation, shooting wildlife on the lake.

Puccini was buried in a tomb inside the villa at Torre del Lago. It seemed rather strange to pass by him there, then see all around the furniture and everyday articles he used. There are many photos on the walls; outside in a small pavilion is a rare collection of some of his manuscripts, letters and memorabilia. His last year was spent in severe pain, and when diagnosed with throat cancer, the doctors placed needles in his throat to try to cure the cancer until the pain caused him to have a heart attack, which resulted in his subsequent death. It is difficult to imagine what agony he must have experienced and one wonders why such a genius had to be subjected to so much horrific pain.

Torre del Lago is the principal remaining shrine to Puccini and each year there is a small festival of his operas held in the open air. How, one wonders, could such dramatic works as *Tosca* and *La Bohème* been composed here?

Puccini, of course, was himself a very emotional man, forced to leave his native Lucca (the nearby city where he was born) because of his seduction of Elvira; she was a married woman with whom he lived out his extraordinarily productive life, marrying her after the death of her husband. His music is about passion, and death, which he portrays as its inevitable result. His characters cannot and do not choose to do other than to live ruled by their instinctive desires, and if death results, they choose it only too willingly. His music soars and carries all before it; the unforgettable melodies and harmonies in his unique style crystallize a longing for the beloved which transcends the

Puccini's villa at Lake Lago

scandal and sheer horror of death and destruction. His characters are heroes and heroines of love: They dare all, risk all, lose all—and are doomed.

How is it that his music conveys so much? Admittedly, the association of ideas derives partly from the librettos, and Puccini himself was very aware of the importance of a good libretto; much of his correspondence over the period in question is about these matters. But the music itself stands apart, haunting, creating indelible impressions of fear and longing. It does not suffice to analyze it technically—as successions of chords, repetitions of themes, and so forth. There is the unique inspiration of genius itself, a genius which owes little to other composers, because of Puccini's individual and unmistakable style.

Individual style was of course nothing new. Purcell, Handel, Mozart—all in the preceding century—had their own clearly recognizable styles within the shared conventions of eighteenth-century music; Puccini however has a more transparently personal style. One can tell little about Handel or what he felt about anything from his music, except that he wrote to please the musically sophisticated audience of his time. But Puccini is different. His music reflects himself more directly; one grasps that the intense feeling in the music expresses what he himself experienced. Perhaps that is why those who visit Torre del Lago are in a way revealing themselves as people who attach importance to passion in its most unequivocal form. Such attitudes have little to do with art or an appreciation of it; they concern the basic feelings of romance and how these feelings have been stimulated and encouraged by Puccini's music—visitors probably know little of his life.

While music is both a craft and an art, like any professional, Puccini was so thoroughly enmeshed in the creation of music that the craft and the skills disappear, even if such skills were consciously invoked when he wrote his great operas. The librettos remain important; we know who wrote them, we know the stories from which they were derived, and we know what importance he attached to them.

A novel is one thing, an opera derived from it is such a totally different creation that they are practically unrelated experiences. Read *La Dame aux Camelias* by Dumas, and then go to see *La Traviata*. Similarly one can read a guidebook about the Torre del Lago area and have no conception of what it feels like to go there and be in the surroundings and the very house where Puccini wrote the famous operas.

To visit Torre del Lago is not merely being transported a hundred years back; it is a place for the imaginative and romantic soul, being lifted into an eternal world where love and passion take precedence over business and leisure, daily life and domestic concerns. Go there and you will not be disappointed if you view it with the right eyes. If there is time, a visit to Lucca is also well worthwhile. The house where Puccini was born is open to the public and the private rooms are fascinating to visit.

When the composer left for Paris in early April 1898, it was to arrange for the premiere of *La Bohème* at the Opera Comique. But the premiere was postponed, forcing Puccini to spend more than two and a half months away from home.

Ill at ease with the French language, he showed little interest in the city or the hectic social life he was forced to lead. "I came into this world to be born in and live in Torre," he wrote to Ferrucio Pagni, "I cry out—as the snow does for the sun, as coffee does for sugar—for the peace of the mountains, the valleys, the greenery, and red sunset." Poetically, he summed up his feelings in a letter written to Alfredo Caselli one month after his arrival in the French capital:

> *I am fed up with Paris. I yearn for the scented woods, with their fragrance, the undulation of my paunch within loose trousers, without a vest. I yearn for the free and fragrant wind that reaches me from the sea. I savour its salty air with dilated nostrils and wide-open lungs.*
>
> *I hate pavements.*
> *I hate large buildings.*
> *I hate capitals.*
> *I hate columns.*
> *I love the beautiful columns of the poplar and the fir; the arches of shaded avenues, there to create my temple, my home, my studio. I love the green expanse of the cool shelter of the woods—old and young. I love the blackbird, the blackcap, the woodpecker. I hate the horse, the cat, the tamed sparrow, the house dog. I hate the steamer, the top hat, the tails . . .*

When he wrote this, the composer was unhappy with the rehearsals, which were more exacting than usual because of the various cast changes which had made the postponements necessary. What upset him was the enormous publicity campaign that involved his attendance at endless receptions where he was introduced to *tout Paris,* which bored him and made him increasingly nervous.

By the spring of 1898 he was more than ready to devote full time to a new opera, particularly after the long fallow period in Paris. To do so, he felt that he needed to find a temporary home away from both Milan and Torre del Lago. Torre del Lago, in addition to its oppressive summer heat, was too filled with friends and the temptation of hunting. To re-create the dark, brooding atmosphere of *Tosca,* he felt the need for total isolation. "I will," he wrote to Illica, "seclude myself in a Lucchese villa, where I will at last rest my forearm on the *toscano* table."

The villa in which Puccini worked that summer belonged to his friend, the Marchese Raffaello Mansi. It was located in the small village of Monsagrati, one of the many tiny villages that dot the hills surrounding Lucca. A stone placed on the side of the Villa Mansi proclaims that it was there that the composer wrote the first act of *Tosca*; it does not state that it was, in effect, a kind of prison for the composer and Elvira. They hated it, but at least Puccini had his work to keep him occupied. The villa was large and comfortable, but the surroundings were ugly and oppressive. The days were blisteringly hot, so hot that the composer was forced to work at night—usually from ten o'clock until four in the morning.

Out in the woods, Puccini had nothing to do but work; few human beings came near the place. Nonetheless, it was just what he wanted, and he planned to stay there until October! That was if he could last and if Elvira could sustain her martyrdom and remain there for that length of time.

In spite of personal discomfort, Puccini's summer had been a productive one, and he almost maintained his promise to remain in the mountain retreat until October, not leaving there until September 22. When he left for Torre del Lago, where he could ease the burden of work with the pleasures of hunting, he was well satisfied with the progress he had made.

The composer was able to stay in Torre until the end of the year, and, as always, it provided him with the breathing space he badly needed. He began working on the second act, and this was, according to notes on the score, completed on July 16. On September 29, the third and final act of *Tosca* was completed.

Relieved that his work had come to an end and confident of its success, Puccini sent the score off to Ricordi. There was no way he could have anticipated the violent response from his publisher and friend, who disliked the opera, especially the third act, stating that as it stood, it "seems to me a serious error of conception and execution." Puccini was stunned by this severe if affectionate rebuke from his publisher.

However he next composed *Madam Butterfly* and became a truly international star. Most of this opera was written at his piano at Torre del Lago.

Chapter Five

Beethoven in Vienna

At school, back in Tasmania, our piano teacher used to enter her more enthusiastic students into the city's local yearly piano competition. So, from around the ages of ten to fourteen, the anticipation and seriousness of these students was intense and extremely competitive. My teacher entered me into the Junior Piano Championship section during the phase when I was practicing Chopin obsessively, but the required piece of music we all had to perform was the first movement of Beethoven's "Moonlight Sonata." Thinking back, I marvel at how the adjudicator could sit through a dozen or so interpretations of this sonata. I mean, how many ways can it be played? It must have made him half crazed.

This was my introduction to Beethoven. All the students loved playing the piece, particularly as it was so easy to play and most of us still remember how to play it. Winning that competition was the forerunner to receiving a scholarship to go to London to study at the Guildhall School. Then, of course, came the concertos and the symphonies. One student was determined not only to play all the sonatas, but to memorize them too, in the space of six months, a feat that impressed all us of tremendously.

When I arrived in London I had an introductory letter to the Tasmanian concert pianist, Eileen Joyce, who was at that time an internationally renowned performer. I met her and she invited me to tea one day in her studio, where we sat and talked about her concert career. She astounded me by saying, "If you can possibly do anything else with your life, do it. The sacrifices and the discipline needed for a concert career are almost too much to bear." She added that even though she was now at the peak of her career, she still had to practice four or five hours a day.

It was a thrill to play one of Beethoven's concertos with the school orchestra at the end of term, although it was a unique challenge. The stage was very crowded, and the piano had been placed so I couldn't see the conductor from the keyboard, so I quickly asked another student to sit under the piano and conduct me from there, or rather at least to keep time with the rest of the players. I had been practicing the work for months, but the young orchestra students had just been given the music, so they were sight reading.

For a time, Beethoven released me from my obsession with Chopin. I listened to the concertos and symphonies with awe. I became passionate about his music and was determined to go to Vienna to see his where he lived and see the city. My first visit was in the autumn, when the Vienna woods were a mass of gold, red and yellow. I found that there were over ninety plaques throughout the city in honor of him, and that he had lived in at least a dozen places there. So I tracked down his birth place, Bonn, and I made a side trip there.

Ludwig van Beethoven was born into a family of court musicians employed at the Archbishop's Palace, situated in Bonn. His grandfather, whose name he bore, was bass singer and Kapellmeister at the electoral court, for the Archbishop; his father, Johann, was a court tenor and music teacher of only moderate talent.

Beethoven's birthplace, at Bongasse 20, had a kitchen and utility room on the ground floor, a cellar underneath, three rooms on the first floor, a couple of tiny attic rooms, and a gorgeous garden; it's now beautifully restored. Ludwig was born in one of the tiny attic rooms on December 15 or 16, 1770, although the event was not recorded at the time and Beethoven, for most of his life, believed that he had been born in December of 1772, not 1770. Perhaps we shall never know the actual date, even though it has been confirmed by official documents that he was baptized on December 17, 1770. Now called the Beethoven-Haus, it has been turned into a museum with the largest Beethoven collection of books, musical artifacts and memorabilia in the world. Visitors will also find a studio containing digital collections and a screen for video clips including a modern production of his only opera, *Fidelio.*

Thanks to his musical family, Beethoven's studies started early. A neighbor relates that his father kept him practicing the clavier "severely." She remembers the older man leading the boy to the clavier, where the youngster had to stand on a small bench to play. The father, who later became an alcoholic, actually seems to have been jealous of the young Beethoven's musical skills. One biographer surmises that he wanted the young man to concentrate on the modest goal of becoming a steady court musician. Once he happened to be playing the violin without sheet music, when his father came in and said, "What is all that silly nonsense you are scraping away so badly? You know that I cannot stand it. Scrape from notes, otherwise all your scraping will not be of any use to you. Stop it, or otherwise I'll box your ears."

Fortunately, the young musician did not follow in his father's and grandfather's footsteps to become a court musician. Instead, when he was old enough, he headed for the musical capital, Vienna, where his first residence was, you might say, "princely." Living in such an abode did not mean that Beethoven had suddenly become affluent; some of the palaces belonging to the nobility took in tenants. As only the main floor (one flight up called the *piano nobile*) was occupied by the owner, other floors were rented out. It was possible for an indigent artisan to rent, for very little, a stuffy dormer room under the roof. Beethoven chose a ground-floor apartment in the residence of Prince Karl Lichnowsky on the Alserstrasse. The Prince grew to like the young man and moved him into his own lodgings and, for many years, was one of his principal supporters.

Here is, perhaps, a good place to mention Beethoven's delusion of grandeur. He allowed the impression that he was of noble birth—attributed to the "van" in his name—to flourish even though some of his personal friends begged him to set the rumor straight. Reports that Beethoven was the illegitimate son of a king of Prussia—variously Friedrich Wilhelm II and Frederick the Great—first appeared in print in 1810, and were repeated in encyclopedias, music dictionaries and music periodicals through the remainder of his lifetime. To many requests from his closest friends to put the matter right, he replied, "You say that I have been mentioned somewhere as being the natural son of the late King of Prussia. Well, the same thing was said to me a long time ago. But I have adopted the principle of neither writing anything about myself nor replying to anything that has been written about me. Hence I gladly leave it to you to make known to the world the integrity of my parents, and especially of my mother." Yet, having written this letter, he neglected to have it posted. Evidently, he still had a powerful resistance to refuting the rumor.

I was personally interested in learning whether Beethoven and Mozart ever met. They did. There is an interesting anecdote about their meeting, which occurred around 1787. It was reported that, at Mozart's request, Beethoven played something for him. Mozart, presuming that it was a show piece prepared for the occasion, praised it in a rather cool manner. Observing this, the young man begged Mozart to give him a theme for improvisation. He always played admirably when excited and now he was inspired, too, by the presence of the master, whom he revered greatly; he played so brilliantly that Mozart's attention and interest grew tremendously. He listened silently, then finally went over to some friends who were sitting in an adjoining room, and said, "Keep your eyes on him. Some day he will give the world something to talk about."

Perhaps another delusion this composer embraced was his ability with women. What many of his biographers dwell at length upon is "The Immortal Beloved." Many of them noticed that, despite being a relatively short man, just five feet, four inches, and with a very nervous disposition, he was very often in love, yet his attachments were very brief. He never married, and it is suggested that these disappointments in love only drove him more ferociously into his music. Be that as it may, the affair with the woman known as "The Immortal Beloved" was of a different order. Found among Beethoven's personal effects after his death was the only unalloyed love letter of his bachelor existence. As one biographer said, it was "an uncontrolled outburst of passionate feeling, exalted in tone, confused in thought, and ridden with conflicting emotions." There was no tinge of amorous charade here; Beethoven, for the first and as far as we know the only time in his life, had found a woman whom he loved and who fully reciprocated his love.

July 6, in the morning.

    My angel, my all, my very self—Only a few words today and at that with pencil (with yours)—Not till tomorrow will my lodgings be definitely determined upon—what a useless waste of time—Why this deep sorrow when necessity speaks—can our love endure except through sacrifices, through not demanding everything from one another; can you change the fact that you are not wholly mine, I not wholly thine . . . My heart is full of so many things to say to you—ah—there are moments when I feel that speech amounts to nothing at all—Cheer up—remain my true, my only treasure, my all as I am yours. The gods must send us the rest, what for us must and shall be—

    Your faithful Ludwig

No less than ten women of the time have been thought by biographers to possibly be "The Immortal Beloved." The puzzle remains unsolved.

I will close with words of someone else who made a pilgrimage in search of Beethoven's spirit, the Chilean pianist, Claudio Arrau. In 1938, in Mexico City, he played all the sonatas and concerti of Beethoven—an artistic consecutive achievement that is without precedent in the history of the piano. Arrau loved to travel to Vienna and, to the best of his ability, he traced the footsteps of Beethoven, either by trying to visit the thirty known Vienna homes of Beethoven, from his move from Bonn in 1792 until his death in 1827, to walks in the woods where the composer wandered and composed. Arrau was once told by the elderly guardian at the small Beethoven museum in the two-story house at 6 Probusgasse that the composer changed his Viennese address seventy-nine times in thirty-five years.

The inspiration Arrau derived from such pilgrimages can be summed up in his notes on the last three sonatas:

> After completing his last three great Sonatas, Opus 109, 110 and 111, Beethoven was able to write to his publisher that 'the pianoforte is, after all, an unsatisfactory instrument.' Considering the works that were going to occupy the remaining years of his life—the Ninth Symphony, the Missa Solemnis and the last five String Quartets, it is an understandable conclusion. It is a conclusion that helps us to understand the enigmatic character of these three sonatas.
>
> When Beethoven can say this about the piano he is saying plainly that he has not succeeded in expressing all he wanted to express and blames it on his instrument. He could not succeed entirely to his satisfaction because in these three works, he attempted to capture the uncapturable—to name the un-nameable. He wanted in them or through them, to be given, and therefore to give, nothing else than the answer to the meaning of life. In Opus 109 and 110, he wages a heroic battle in the deep regions of his soul and strains at the walls that enclose him. He breaks up old forms and discovers new ones, and finally at the end of Opus 111, he can see the clear stars of heaven again. After these works, after these gigantic battles on the ground of his personal means

of expression—the pianoforte—could come the renewed affirmation of life—the final yes to life he was searching for and which he gives us so overwhelmingly in the choral conclusion of the Ninth Symphony.

Volumes have been written speculating about how Beethoven could still compose after losing his hearing, of how he used to drum the piano with his hand, to feel the vibrations of the rhythm of what he was composing. This was after he had become deaf. The notes, chords and progressions were all in his head so he didn't have to hear them. He knew what the violins would sound like if he superimposed the woodwinds on them. His genius was not only for composing but in being able to write music down without hearing the many dramatic crescendos or the finale of the last movement of a symphony.

Two of the most memorable traits of Beethoven were his sadness and his sense of humor. To Johann Hummel, who visited him on his deathbed, he joked about Hummel's wife. "You are a lucky man," he said with a smile. "You have a wife who takes care of you, who is in love with you—but poor me." And then he sighed heavily. Later, realizing the imminence of death and having signed his last will and testament, he turned to two of his friends and said, "Applaud, friends, the play is finished." A little later a special shipment of four bottles of wine arrived. Upon their presentation Beethoven murmured, "Pity, pity, too late!" According to a witness, the day was very cold; snow had fallen. Around five o'clock a sudden thunderstorm obscured the sky. It became very dark. Suddenly there was a great flash of lightning that illuminated the death chamber, accompanied by violent claps of thunder. With the lightning, Beethoven opened his eyes, raised his tightly clenched right hand, and fell back dead. It was about 5:15 p.m., March 26, 1827. One biographer notes that one thinks of the lines from Julius Caesar:

When beggars die, there are no comets seen;
The heavens themselves blaze forth the death of princes.

In Grillparzer's funeral oration he says,

Thus he was, thus he died, thus will he live for all time!

And you who have followed our escort to this place, hold your sorrow in sway. You have not lost him but have won him. No living man enters the halls of immortality. The body must die before the gates are opened. He whom you mourn is now among the greatest men of all time, unassailable for ever. Return to your homes, then, distressed but composed. And whenever, during your lives, the power of his works overwhelms you like a coming storm; when your rapture pours out in the midst of a generation yet unborn; then remember this hour and think: we were there when they buried him, and when he died we wept!

Noël Coward at Waterloo

Chapter Six

Noël Coward in London, New York and Jamaica

Following in Noël Coward's Footsteps

When we were young, my brother and I used to go down to the docks in Hobart to watch the great ocean liners arrive from overseas. It was something to do after school. The feeling of awe at the size of these ships, the mystery of far-flung ports of call, and the lure of the sea captured our hearts, but we never dreamed that one day we would sail on one of them. I had begun collecting pictures and brochures about the ships' histories. We could walk right up to the front of their bows. The dream from childhood of sailing to a far-off location remained firmly implanted in my psyche. Later, when I was living in London, there would be photos of celebrities in the daily newspapers, leaving Waterloo or Victoria station by the famous boat train to catch one of these ships in Southampton. Friends and family would go to the station to say farewell to these stars and it all seemed very glamorous and exciting. When I read about Coward sailing across the Atlantic to New York, and meeting so many illustrious passengers on board, I was determined to follow in his footsteps and to visit all the places he wrote about. I had acted in his plays and was passionate about his wonderfully witty songs, from "Mad Dogs and Englishmen," and "I Went to a Marvelous Party," to "I'll See You Again" and "A Room with a View." He wrote about his times in New York in his diaries. He knew many theatre people and had very close friends in Manhattan. It seemed like he went everywhere! But after his pleasant crossing to New York, all was not so easy when he arrived. He dreamed of having his name in lights on Broadway, as some of us still do. But let's find out about his first journey.

◆ ◆ ◆

It was with the glamorous image of New York in his mind, and with his name in lights on Broadway as his most heartfelt wish, that Coward traveled, on a Cunard liner (naturally!) across the Atlantic, accompanied by an aristocratic English friend, Jeffrey Amherst, in May 1921. The liner *Aquitania* seemed to symbolize the glamorous world that Coward was convinced was his by right, but fate gave him a warning of the trials ahead when many of the ship's crew—including, vitally, the cooks—went on strike! Having survived this example of backstage rebellion, Coward caught his first glimpse of Manhattan on a gorgeous June morning.

Even today, the experience of gliding past the skyscrapers and docks of New York is exciting, however often one may have had it, but to a young man in the early 1920s it must have been especially breathtaking. A stickler for doing things well and aiming for the best, Coward made straight for the Algonquin Hotel, but he could barely wait to deliver his suitcases before rushing off to Broadway. Noël had theatre in the blood: not for nothing was he the author of "The Boy Actor," a superb and moving poem about a child actor whose formative years were spent, not on the games field but on stage. Not for him were the cheers of his fellows as he scored a goal—his adrenaline surged not on muddy fields but with the smell of greasepaint, the tattered glamour of theatre dressing rooms, the sound of the front-of-house orchestra, and the thrill of an extra curtain call.

Coward's delight in Broadway reflects the fact that, for all the British pride in London's theatreland, even the most patriotic of British actors (and Noël Coward, after all, wrote that love song to the city, "London Pride," at the height of the Second World War) realized that Broadway was somewhere special; not just because of the traditions of its stately theatres (many of which were as old as anything London had to offer, after all), but because of the sheer electricity in the air and on the billboards, which used the latest marketing techniques to make the desirable seem impossible to miss.

The excitement that was a hallmark of Broadway was also reflected in the hectic social life of the city, particularly among the rather more adventurous theatrical set. Coward made many new friends and bumped into chums from London who, like him, had come to America in search of dollars. This change from usual Edwardian practice—when rich American girls would come to England in search of titles and all the grander appurtenances of "class"—marked a sea-change that the First World War had created. Although Britain had won the war and survived the revolutions that swept the continent, it was already clear to those with foresight that this was to be the American Century. During this first stay in New York, Noël's success proved to be more elusive than he expected, and his accommodations, which had started so grandly at the Algonquin, slipped progressively downward to ever more humble abodes. He was thrown a lifeline by Gabrielle Enthoven, who gave him a room in her flat on the understanding that he would pay rent when and if he sold a play. A theatre enthusiast, she left a vast collection of theatre memorabilia to the Theatre Museum, Covent Garden.

While trying to break into Broadway, Noël met two vitally important friends, Alfred Lunt and Lynn Fontanne, for whom he wrote, and with whom he costarred in *Design for Living* some years later, when all three were safely successful. The play has been sporadically revived since the 1930s but is primarily of interest for its biographical background rather than its artistic merit. In 1995, a revival was staged at the Globe Theatre (now renamed the Gielgud, in honor of Sir John Gielgud). I found it hard to really sympathize with any of the three characters; their bisexual love tangle was not so much daring as passé.

While his acting work was in abeyance, Noël wrote stories which he was able to sell, including to *Vanity Fair*. This provided him with periodic bursts of income, but he had to cut his cloth according to his means, so instead of the lavish lunches that he would later so greatly enjoy, he dined in less than splendor at an Italian deli on MacDougal Street. When eating at home, bereft of air-conditioning, and in the full blast of a New York summer, he prepared his food stark naked, unaware that his anatomy was easily viewed by passersby and neighbors. In one of those famous incidents that swiftly became part of Noël Coward folklore, he was called on by a bad-tempered policeman, whose indignation was quickly overcome—despite the obvious disadvantage—by Noël's extraordinary charm. Aided, one suspects, by the fact that the charm was accompanied by half a bottle of wine, the policeman supposedly not only left Noël to his own devices but gave him his revolver, as the neighborhood was notoriously dangerous. It makes a great story, but one can't help thinking that the likelihood of a hardened precinct cop handing over his revolver to a strange, naked Englishman, let alone leaving it at his apartment, beggars belief. Mind you, quite a lot of Coward's "career" was distinctly larger than life.

Coward teamed up with another larger-than-life Englishman who was in New York at the time—Ronald Colman, who was soon to have the most famous little moustache since Charlie Chaplin, though at the time was as much a penniless hopeful as Coward himself. Noël overcame his lack of money as he did all obstacles—with charm and determination. Accounts of his time in New York, therefore, alternate between accounts of poverty (having to borrow money from Lynn Fontanne, for example) and descriptions of society parties on the Upper East Side and in country houses, at least one of which was thought to have been the inspiration for *Hay Fever,* one of his most successful comedies. When he left for England, as the leaves began to fall in Central Park, Noël Coward had failed to make the professional breakthrough he had anticipated, but he had launched himself on the social scene and was confident—and determined—that he would return. The fact that he did return throughout his career was evidence of the two-way love affair between Coward and New York. On his second visit, in 1924, his songs were performed in Andre Charlot's *Revue of 1924*—a show that may not have had a very exciting title (though its starry cast included Jack Buchanan and Gertrude Lawrence) but became a hit as the Charlot revues caught the mood of the age. It is easy, at this distance, to forget that memories of the First World War were still very much in people's minds. The hedonism of the 1920s was a reaction to the horrors of the war, and this was a period when the well-to-do had the resources to live well and dine late. Revues were the perfect entertainment for smart New York (and London) society—clever and amusing yet easily digestible. Pictures taken at the time show the audiences to have been beautifully and formally dressed, determined to have a glamorous night out. They would have been astonished had they seen the dressing down that generally takes place today, particularly in London. New York audiences, by and large, are much better dressed than West End ones.

During his 1924 stay, Noël began at the Ritz Hotel, on Madison Avenue, but decided to economize by moving to a friend's flat on East 32nd Street. When he returned to the city in 1926, he again started out at the Ritz but swiftly decided that the place was too expensive, so moved to the Gladstone on East 52nd Street—a smart, simpler base from which to operate.

He was in New York for the opening of his play, *This Was a Man,* but the rehearsals went so badly (as was often the case with his productions) that he decamped to Long

Island. When the play opened on November 22, it was a failure. The old theatrical adage that a disastrous dress rehearsal meant a successful first night was not proved true on this occasion. Coward quipped to a friend that the actors' delivery was so plod-dingly slow that there was time to pop out and get an ice cream between each line!

Noël's next visit, in 1928, was a reconnaissance mission. During a two-week stay, he took the opportunity to catch up with all the latest shows. On arrival he checked into the Ritz (of course!) and gave a press interview, in which he claimed that he felt perfectly at home in New York, and that its theatre-going public were much friendlier and more enthusiastic than those in London. Even allowing for a little judicious buttering up of the local newspapers, Noël had put his finger on a truth that still holds good—Americans enjoy and applaud success, while the English are extremely wary of it. The English sympathy is invariably with the plucky underdog, rather than the tri-umphal winner, and they don't really give themselves over to stars until those stars are old and safely past their prime; then it is considered good form to admire them. A clas-sic example of this is Dame Gracie Fields, who had plenty of problems during her prime, particularly during the Second World War when she was married to an Italian citizen; yet she was trundled out on stage to tumultuous applause and genuine affec-tion when she was an old lady.

The frenetic pace, the flaunting of wealth, the sense of fun that characterized the New York of the 1920s was shattered by the Wall Street crash in 1929. The knock-on effect reverberated around the world and was reflected in the theatre as well as other spheres of life. Noël was still writing comedies (most notably, of course, *Private Lives*), but there was an added depth and maturity to his work, as well as a sense of nostalgia and foreboding. *Cavalcade* was a patriotic tribute to the past, but also a warning about the future, a suggestion that there might be another disaster (there is a scene on board a doomed ocean liner in the show) looming ahead.

Atlantic liners continued to convey Noël safely over the waves, however, and he chose to commemorate this international lifestyle by naming a production company, set up in the early 1930s, Trans-Atlantic Presentations. Realizing the good sense of owning his own place in New York, he bought an apartment on East 52nd Street, but his stay there (in 1936) was brief, as he suffered one of his periodic nervous break-downs. These were a characteristic of his career, and were, in a sense, a safety valve. He was so full of ideas, of energy, and of a ruthless determination to succeed that he lived life at a pace and intensity far greater than most of his contemporaries—which is, perhaps, why we remember him while they are long since forgotten.

It was to recover from these personal crises that he traveled abroad so often and in the luxury and calm of ocean liners. Given that he divided his career between two of the greatest cities on earth, and given the phenomenal pace of life in New York, which was then, and still remains, the most exciting and vibrant metropolis on the planet, it is little wonder that these much-needed holidays occurred so frequently.

When the world hit its equivalent of a collective breakdown, with the outbreak of the Second World War, Noël sailed to New York in order to arouse sympathy and support for Britain. He left for America in April 1940, shortly before the invasion and fall of France, which would leave Britain to face Nazi Germany and its allies alone. Officially, he was there to promote a new play (after all, the United States was a neutral country at the time), but the reality was that he was to be a one-man propaganda mission for England (reminiscent of his friend and fellow-composer/playwright, Ivor Novello, who had been sent to Stockholm—Sweden was a neutral country during the First World War). The fact that he was able to enjoy unrationed food and a pre-war lifestyle in New York, which were then only memories in London, was an added attraction.

The war years saw Noël working in England and touring the Empire, with morale-boosting concerts for the troops. Once the war had been safely won, however, he returned to America, but his *Tonight at 8.30* was not the success he had hoped for. The late 1940s and the 1950s were a very fallow period for Coward. Tastes had changed, the world had changed, and in many ways he seemed dated and out of touch. His big post-war musical, *Pacific 1860,* starring Mary Martin, was a flop. What could he do? As the 1950s wore on, he had the added problem of income tax problems; the Labour Government that had been elected by a landslide in 1945 had raised taxes to fund a socialist transformation of the country. Noël was an unashamed Conservative and was appalled by both government politics as well as its economics, but it was the latter that hit the hardest.

What was he to do? At a time when America was at the height of its economic boom, it seemed that it might, as it had thirty years earlier, be a launching pad for his career. The growth of television (which was still relatively rare in England—it took the Queen's coronation in 1953 to kick-start it as a popular pastime in the United Kingdom) seemed to offer a solution, and Noël seized the opportunity with both

Blue Harbour, Coward (on the steps) with friends

hands. He may have grown older and statelier, but at heart he was still the ambitious, determined man who had climbed from lower-middle-class obscurity to international fame and fortune.

Most of the money that Noël made in America came from cabaret performances in Las Vegas, and there is a famous record cover showing him standing, dressed in a tuxedo, in the Nevada desert. The idea for this work came from his having introduced Marlene Dietrich at the Café de Paris in London. If a huge star like her could, after the war, reinvent herself as a cabaret star, representing pre-war glamour and style, then so, in his way, could he.

In addition to his Las Vegas cabaret appearances, however, he also appeared on New York television for CBS. And it was in New York that he met the producer Mike Todd—also the husband of Elizabeth Taylor. Todd persuaded him to take a part in the movie *Around the World in Eighty Days* which starred David Niven, another Englishman revered for his Old World glamour and gentlemanly disposition. This was, sadly, to be Todd's only film, as he was killed in a plane crash not long after.

During the production of the TV show, Noël stayed in an apartment on East 54th Street—it had taken twenty years to move two streets farther uptown toward the Upper East Side! The show, called *Together with Music,* was a great success, even though (or perhaps because) he had toned down some of the sexier lines in some of his songs, in deference to the rather more puritanical nature of American television audiences.

Tax troubles had led to Noël's working in America. Having no intention of leading an impoverished old age, he decided to become a tax exile. Much as he loved America, taxwise it was not the best place for him to live, so he bought homes in Bermuda (of which he tired) and then Switzerland, as well as his beloved home, Firefly, in Jamaica. It was while en route to Jamaica that he made his last ever journey to New York, in January 1973, to see a production of *Oh Coward.* Fittingly, he made his final public appearance there, with his old friend Marlene Dietrich. After a week's residence in New York, he traveled on to Jamaica, where he died, two months later.

One of the best recordings available of Noël Coward performing his work is a CD called *The Noël Coward Album.* Suitably, it is made up of recordings made during performances in the States, in both Las Vegas and in his beloved New York. His attitude toward the States was summed up in the song, "I Like America," but his love of New York could best be described, I feel, in the words of one of his comedy numbers: "I Went to a Marvelous Party." If Noël's spirit lives on, one of the places he is surely to be found is at an after-theatre party in the heart of Manhattan.

"Men go to the theatre to forget; women, to remember. In the theatre, a hero is one who believes that all women are ladies, a villain, one who believes all ladies are women."
—George Jean Nathan, *The Theatre*

Blue Harbour

It has just been announced that Noël Coward's house in Jamaica, "Blue Harbour," is up for sale as is his old place in London. However, what is unique about his Jamaica home is that most of his original furniture, books and photographs are still there. Also, it is a very well kept secret that his home is a reasonably priced guesthouse. This is where Coward entertained guests including Cecil Beaton, Celia Johnson, Ian Fleming and many other celebrities.

However, the owners have decided to sell, which seems such a shame considering the history of the house. When I stayed there last year, I was given Coward's old bedroom and slept in his four-poster bed at the top of the house, looking out on a magnificent view of the ocean. I sat at his desk, where he wrote so many of his plays and songs. His piano was in the room beside it. The current owners bought the house from Coward's companion, Cole Lesley, after Coward's death, so they have kept it as it was

Blue Harbour, author to the left of the steps, with its current owners

Elizabeth Sharland at the piano at Firefly

in those days. Included in the sale are the two little guest villas in the garden. They also have the original furniture, with a mirrored art deco dressing table, which he bought for Marlene Dietrich, and the two-bedroom villa where the Oliviers stayed, as well as the Lunts, Katharine Hepburn, Joan Sutherland and Clifton Webb.

The swimming pool is on the edge of the sea so that fresh sea water can be pumped in and out of it regularly. The pretty walk through the garden leads you to the private beach farther along the seven-acre property. If any theatre historian or Coward fan would like to stay in Coward's home, this is the time to do it, before it is sold. It is the only Coward property where you can spend a night and experience the joy that Coward had when living there. Nothing has been changed; even the little shower stalls with the original tiles are still the same, as are the wood floors and window shutters.

Coward wrote about his time there in his diaries and how he decided to build a smaller house up on the hill behind Blue Harbour. He called it Firefly and moved there a few years later on his own. However, he did entertain the Queen Mother there for lunch one day. He gave her two bullshots (vodka and bouillon), but the lobster bisque he had made wouldn't defrost in time . . . he said it had the consistency of Slazenger tennis balls, so at the last minute he had to make a soup. Nevertheless, the Queen Mother was delighted and stayed for three hours. The drive from Kingston, by one of the three drivers who work at Blue Harbour, takes about two hours via the scenic route, which takes you through the Blue Mountains. The other route is from Montego Bay by the new highway and passes Goldeneye, the former home of Ian Fleming (creator of James Bond), whose marriage Coward attended in the tiny church in the local nearby town of St. Maria. Reading in Coward's diaries the names of the legendary theatre celebrities is like reading *Who's Who in Theatre*.

George Bernard Shaw

Chapter Seven

George Bernard Shaw in Ayot St. Lawrence

Anyone who has ever read or seen a play by George Bernard Shaw is usually curious to read more about the man. His works are still as popular today as they were in his day, although perhaps he is not talked about quite so much at present. Every few years another writer publishes another biography of him, since he is one of England's best-known playwrights, up there with Shakespeare. Ever since I acted in *St. Joan* years ago, I have had memories of other great actresses who had played her, from Sybil Thorndike to Trevor Nunn's wife, Imogen Stubbs. Any actor who plays a lead in a Shaw play remembers the effect that one of his plays has on an audience. St. Joan is a marvelous part, but then so are many wonderful Shaw roles for women, including Liza in *Pygmalion,* originated by Wendy Hiller.

The late Barry Morse, who was president of the prestigious Shaw Society in England, probably knew more about Shaw's life than anyone, except perhaps Michael Holroyd, who wrote a four-volume Shaw biography several years ago. When I wrote the book *The British on Broadway,* Barry kindly supplied the Foreword to the book, since he was a theatre historian as well as a Broadway and West End actor.

I passionately wanted to see where Shaw lived, because everyone wrote about what a simple and almost monastic life he led at Ayot. He was a vegetarian and also a nondrinker, who believed in physical exercise, and clearly, cold baths and no central heating. He and his wife, Charlotte, whom he married late, lived there until the end of their lives. It is a well-known fact that their marriage was not consummated and that Charlotte was more of a helpmate, companion and secretary.

He had a small wooden hut constructed in the garden, where he could work in private without distractions from the house, although he did have a telephone extension put in, to be used only in emergencies. The hut was built so that it could be turned slowly to follow the sun, whenever there was sun, as he was working. This little building is still there, as are his desk and chair and small daybed. I was fascinated to stand there, at the door of the hut, alone, the only sound that of the birds in the nearby tree, and imagine how many hours, days, years he wrote inside this tiny space. I imagined him being there and wished I could talk to him, although I think he would have told me to bugger off.

The day I visited the house and grounds, I was the only visitor, so I was granted some privileges. I was allowed to play his small upright piano and sit down in his living room, which still contained many of his books and furniture. The dining room was sparse and very cold. I couldn't imagine the two Shaws, seated there without heat, meat or wine!

The kitchen was just as cold and severe. It must have been extremely bitter in the winter months. The exterior of the red brick house is really quite ugly and gives the impression of a schoolhouse almost, with very small windows and not much of a view. The gardens are better, especially in the back of the house. There is a large lawn and flowerbeds beyond it, as well as a fair number of trees. Many of his guests who visited him there wrote of how well he looked but how difficult it was to find the house. He also kept a flat in London, from which he would drive up to Ayot each weekend. Years later he gave up his London home and remained in the country.

Each year at Ayot, around the anniversary of his birthday, there is a mini Shaw Festival with a company of actors presenting one or two of his short plays in the garden at the back of the house, with the actors using the doors for the entrances and exits, and one suddenly imagines that Shaw himself might come through one of the doors to take a bow after the play ends. It is a charming festival. People bring their own baskets of food and picnic on the lawn facing the back of the house, bringing their own little tables or eating on the grass. Bottles of wine appear, and as the sun sets on a summer evening, the place becomes quite magical. Every year the Shaw Society fosters new talent—the actors love the environment and the inspiration of acting in the playwright's garden.

Shaw was amazingly prolific. He wrote not only plays, books and articles, but also corresponded with hundreds of people, so it is a wonder he found the time to entertain at all. He loved writing to actresses who were playing in his plays, and fell in love with at least two of them, Ellen Terry and Mrs. Patrick Campbell, or "Stella," as he nicknamed her.

I wrote a play called *The Private Life of GBS,* featuring Shaw as well as eleven women he was directly associated with, though not all at one time. Barry Morse produced it at the Theatre Museum in London with eleven women, he himself played GBS in his Norfolk jacket and Irish accent. We also did a reading at the Algonquin Hotel in New York, with Barrie Ingham playing Shaw, and Rosemary Harris, Carol Higgins Clark and Arlene Stern. The play explains the dilemma Shaw had in meeting Ellen Terry. He wrote to her almost every day but never met her. One evening she looked through the peephole in the curtain on stage and caught a glimpse of him. He was also writing almost every day to Mrs. Patrick Campbell and his letters to her are still in print.

Shaw's Corner, Ayot St. Lawrence

He lived at that time with his mother in Tavistock Square, but they rarely ate together or saw each other, even though they occupied the same house. He was racing from one political meeting to another and neglecting himself and his health. His foot became infected and he didn't bother the bandage it properly, so it got worse. He needed a secretary and began wondering if he was going to survive the workload and keep his health. Friends suggested Charlotte Payne Townsend for this position, though when she came for an interview she was appalled. She described his room as completely chaotic. Heaps of letters, pages of manuscripts, books, knives, forks, spoons, sometimes a cup of cocoa, or a half finished plate of porridge, a saucepan, and a dozen other things were mixed up indiscriminately and all undusted because he said that his papers must not be touched. "I knew something had to be done," she remarked. Later on, after she had got to know him, and she realized that his mother couldn't take care of him or herself, she offered to find a place in the country and take charge, but not without marriage.

He was too ill to go out and get a ring and a license, but asked her to do so. He then wrote that he found that his own objection to marriage had ceased with his objection to his own death. Charlotte settled an annuity on his mother, as she couldn't afford to keep herself, and had become rather neurotic, turning to ouija boards and séances in keeping with her ideas on the unseen forces beyond the material world.

So, the couple were married in Henrietta Street in Covent Garden. Shaw wrote:

> We were married on June 1st in a registry office. It was pouring with rain. Of the two witnesses we had, Sydney Olivier, who was much better dressed than I, was mistaken for the groom and because of my rather shabby attire, I was thought of as someone off the street who'd been called in as a witness. This prompted Charlotte to buy me new clothes. I was a married man at last.

Shortly after they moved into the country house, Shaw, who was using crutches, fell down the staircase and broke his foot, which meant more time on crutches and time in bed.

Charlotte wrote that she felt jealous only of Stella Campbell. Much of Shaw's philandering filled him with shame and disgust, but it did not cure him. It came easily

Barry Morse, past president of the Shaw Society

and naturally to him, as it does to many Irishmen, and he readily and irresistibly appealed to English women unaccustomed to Irish Blarney. He said he was surprised when English women took his flatteries and courtesies and endearments for serious intentions instead of lighthearted attentions he meant them to be. So, often, he had to hastily reverse his engines. However he learned to put his philandering to severely practical uses and to employ it as a means of obtaining, first, the interest, then the goodwill, and finally the cooperation and services of famous actresses. He succeeded.

What he was trying to do was both human and natural. Shaw wrote that he thought marriage is an acquired taste, like "olives or eating winkles with a pin," and thought perhaps that he ought never to have been married. He wrote that some of his most gratifying relationships with women were on paper. "Let those who complain that it was all on paper know that only on paper has humanity achieved truth, beauty, virtue and abiding love."

His sister Lucy often visited, even though she thought he was rather weird, saying that he wouldn't eat meat or touch alcohol. He was quite determined to forego roast lamb for vegetables. "He will become a head full of brains and underneath he will be all woolly underwear and vegetables."

Two of the passions of George Bernard Shaw (apart from his women whom he preferred to keep between the sheets, paper that is, not bedsheets) were undoubtedly music and religion. One of the earliest musical influences on young Shaw was a man named George John Lee, a music teacher and organizer of concerts, who taught Shaw's mother. He then became involved with her and eventually lived with the family in Dublin and later London. Lee moved in with the family when Shaw was seven. Detesting her husband, whom she called a failure and a drunkard, Lee became her new center of gravity. According to Shaw, who wrote about him much later in life, Lee was a man of "mesmeric vitality and force." As a teacher of singing, Lee claimed he could make his young lady students sing "like Patti" (a famous diva of the time) in twelve lessons—at a guinea a lesson.

The introduction of Lee into the Shaw household dramatically increased the young man's interest in music. It was through Lee that music became a dominating influence in his life. By the time he was a teenager he could sing and whistle, from beginning to end, the leading works by Handel, Haydn, Mozart, Beethoven, Rossini and Verdi.

When the Shaw family, minus the father George Carr Shaw, moved with Lee to London, George junior was seventeen. He stayed with his father in Dublin for three years, then moved to London himself to live with his mother, his two sisters, and Lee, who had renamed himself Vandeleur Lee. The London in which the shy, beardless youth arrived in 1876 was very much the gaslit city of Sherlock Holmes. Charles Dickens had only been dead five years. In the same year, Edison was contemplating the idea of recording sound on a revolving cylinder, and twelve months later the phonograph became a reality. Two years later electric light was established and the age of gaslight came to an end.

In London, Shaw began ghost-writing music reviews for Lee for a publication called *The Hornet*. His criticisms were so severe that Lee (under whose name the reviews appeared) was fired. His next journalistic endeavors in music writing came

No. 29, Shaw's home in Tavistock Square

when a tall, restrained Scot of his own age, William Archer, obtained work for Shaw as music critic for *The Dramatic Review* and *The Magazine of Music*. Meanwhile, he was writing his youthful, and not very successful novels, one of them being *Love Among the Artists,* the hero of which is a British Beethoven named Owen Jack, whom Shaw described as utterly unreasonable and unaccountable, "but a vital genius, powerful in an art that is beyond logic and even beyond words."

Some years later Shaw was able to write, "I could make deaf stockbrokers read my two pages on music . . . the alleged joke being that I knew nothing about it. The real joke was that I knew all about it."

In 1888, when Shaw was thirty-two, T. P. O'Connor founded *The Star* and invited Shaw, who was now a Socialist, to join the political staff of his new paper. When he read Shaw's first article, he told him that it would be five hundred years before such radical stuff could be acceptable as political journalism. But, unwilling to sack a fellow Irishmen, the new editor offered him a column on music, with the stipulation that he not write anything about Bach in B Minor. Typically, Shaw's first review began, "The number of empty seats at the performance of Bach's Mass in B Minor at St. James's Hall on Saturday did little credit to the artistic culture of which the West End is supposed to be the universal center . . ."

He wrote for *The Star* under the pseudonym Corno di Bassetto, meaning a basset horn. Soon after joining the paper's staff, Shaw was summoned to the editor's office. "The fact is, my dear Corno," Shaw recalled being told, "I don't believe that music in London is confined to St. James's Hall, Covent Garden and the Albert Hall. People must sing and play elsewhere . . ." So, in his next review, Shaw wrote:

> A little later the train was rushing through the strangest places: Shoreditch, of which I had read in historical novels; Old Ford, which I had supposed to be a character in one of Shakespeare's plays; Homerton, which is associated in my mind with pigeons; and Haggerston, a name perfectly new to me. When I got into the concert room I was perfectly dazzled by the appearance of the orchestra. Nearly all the desks for the second violins were occupied by ladies: beautiful young ladies. Personal beauty is not a strong point of West End orchestras, and I thought the change an immense improvement

until the performance began, when the fair fiddlers rambled from bar to bar with a sweet indecision that had a charm of its own, but was not exactly what Purcell and Handel meant.

He ends his review with the comment,

I am, on the whole, surprised and delighted with the East End, and shall soon venture there without my revolver.

Shaw's approach to religion also had an irreverent edge to it. Perhaps this started with his father who, despite being a self-effacing nonentity, bequeathed his son the sense of anti-climactic humor. Shaw recalls,

When I scoffed at the Bible, my father quite sincerely rebuked me, telling me with what little sternness was in his nature, that I should not speak so; that no educated man would make such a display of ignorance; that the Bible was universally recognized as a literary and historical masterpiece; and as much more to the same effect as he could muster. But when he had reached the point of feeling really impressive, a convulsion of internal chuckling would wrinkle up his eyes; and (I knowing all the time what was coming) would cap his eulogy by assuring me, with an air of perfect fairness, that even the worst enemy of religion could say no worse of the Bible than that it was the damndest parcel of lies ever written.

Shaw also recalls how they were once visited by a Unitarian. When he asked his father what a Unitarian was, George Carr Shaw explained that a Unitarian was one who did not believe that Jesus was crucified, in that he was observed running down the far side of the hill of Calvary.

There is a lot of humor but also deep intellectual curiosity in Shaw's writing about religion. He wrote five plays that he considered religious: *Back to Methuselah, Androcles and the Lion, Saint Joan* (for which he won the Nobel Prize and which many people consider his best play), *The Simpleton of the Unexpected Isles* and *The Adventures of the*

Shaw, writing in his garden shed

Black Girl in Her Search for God. The latter, in which he has this young lady meeting all sorts of people who say they are God, got him into a lot of trouble with a very dear friend, Dame Laurentia McLachlan, a Benedictine nun who became the Abbess of Stanbrook Abbey in England. Writing to her in a discussion about St. Joan, he wrote,

My dear Sister Laurentia, in reading heathen literature like mine, you must remember that I am addressing an audience not exclusively Catholic, it included not only Protestants but also Indians and Orientals. If I wrote from an exclusively Catholic point of view my book would reach no further than the penny lives of the saints which they sell in the Churches of Ireland. I want my sound to go out into all lands!

But he went too far when he sent her his new work, *The Black Girl*. Dame McLachlan wrote to him, "If you had written against my father or my mother, you would not expect to be forgiven or received until you had made amends. I implore you to suppress this book and retract its blasphemies." Shaw wrote back to her in protest, but she did not reply. Over a year later he received through the post a small buff-colored card, with the inscription "In Memory of September 6th, 1884–1934. Dame Laurentia McLachlan, Abbess of Stanbrook."

Shaw penned the following.

To the Ladies of Stanbrook Abbey, Worcester. Dear Sisters, I have just received the news of the death of Dame Laurentia McLachlan. I had no knowledge of the state of her health and no suspicion that I should never see her again on this earth. There was a time when I was in such grace with her that she asked you all to pray for me; and I valued your prayers most sincerely. I wrote a little book which, to my grief, shocked Dame Laurentia so much that I dared not show my face at the Abbey until I was forgiven. She has, I am sure, forgiven me now; but I wish she could tell me so. In the outside world, from which you have escaped, it is sometimes necessary to shock people violently to make them think seriously about religion; and my ways were too rough. I have no right to your prayers; but if I should occasionally be remembered by those of you who recall my old visits I should be none the worse for them, and very grateful. Yours faithfully, G. Bernard Shaw.

In a strange, ironic twist, the small buff-colored card was not to commemorate Dame McLachlan's death, but merely a souvenir of her Golden Jubilee in the

Benedictine habit. But it broke their silence and they remained friends for years to come.

Earlier in their friendship, Shaw announced that he was in fact to become "a pilgrim." He announced to her that he was going to visit Jerusalem. Dame Laurentia girlishly asked him to bring back a little memento from Calvary. At the conclusion of his trip, Shaw wrote:

> You asked me for a relic from Calvary—but Calvary is only a spot on the church pavement, jealously guarded, and with nothing removable about it. Where the real Calvary is nobody knows; for the hills outside the city are innumerable. The alleged Via Dolorosa I traversed in a motor car hooting furiously at the children to get out of my way. So off I went to Bethlehem; and from the threshold of the Church of the Nativity, I picked up a little stone, a scrap of limestone rock that certainly existed when the feet of Jesus pattered about on it and the feet of Mary pursued him to keep him in order. In fact I picked up two little stones: one to be thrown blindfold among the others in Stanbrook garden so that there may always be a stone from Bethlehem there, and nobody will know which it is and be tempted to steal it, and the other for your own self.

Their mutual friend, Sir Sydney Cockerell, Director of the Fitzwilliam Museum in Cambridge, observed that there was no inscription on the reliquary containing the stones. He asked, "Wouldn't it be a good idea to put a brief inscription explaining its purpose and saying who it's from?"

Shaw replied:

> Cockerell is a heathen atheist: a reliquary is no more to him than a football cup. What the devil—saving your cloth—could we put on it? We couldn't put our names on it—could we? That seems to me perfectly awful. "An inscription explaining its purpose!" If we could explain its purpose we could explain the universe. I couldn't. Could you? If Cockerell thinks he can—and he's quite capable of it—let

him try, and submit the result to the Pope. Dear Sister: our finger-prints are on the stone, and Heaven knows whose footprints may be on it. Isn't that enough?

Yes, I think it is safe to say that, in the realms of music and religion, George Bernard Shaw was indeed a passionate pilgrim.

Katherine Mansfield

Chapter Eight

Katherine Mansfield in Menton

Katherine Mansfield was a New Zealand writer who was born in 1888 and died in 1920 at the age of thirty-two. In 1905 she went to England to study the cello. She remained in London after she gave up trying to become a musician, and she began writing short stories that are still much read today. She became a member of the Bloomsbury group, making friends with Virginia Woolf, Lady Ottoline Morrell, Bertrand Russell, D. H. Lawrence and many of the writers of that period. She fell in love with the writer John Middleton Murry and they lived together in London. However Katherine developed tuberculosis and her doctor advised her to spend the winters in a warmer climate. He suggested Morocco or farther south, but said if that was impossible, then the south of France would do. She decided on Bandol, then Menton, which was an unfortunate choice because it was one of the worst places she could go to cure the disease because of the damp atmosphere.

After I read her letters to John Middleton Murry written from the south of France, I was impressed by what a romantic writer she was. Her descriptions of the town of Bandol and of Menton were so vivid I wanted to see for myself where she lived and worked there, and to follow in her footsteps through the palm trees and the pine woods. Her letters were full of descriptions of her walks. Virginia Woolf had written that she was jealous of Mansfield's work, and for that reason didn't read her, even though they had been friends.

Being from New Zealand, she was in constant fear that she would have to return there if things didn't work out in Europe. Already she had been back once, where she was very unhappy and restless and begged her father to let her return, which he did, giving her a small allowance to live on. After she had been diagnosed with tuberculosis, she risked her relationship with John Middleton Murry, leaving him to try to recover from her illness by following the sun and staying in the south of France. During her stay there, she not only wrote short stories but began a long correspondence with Murry who could not, or would not leave England, except for one visit to see her. In 1915 she wrote to him from Menton, "This place is so full of our love that every little walk I take is a passionate pilgrimage."

She had two disastrous marriages, one of which only lasted one day. Her adolescent bisexuality, her illness, her love affairs and her quick wit brings to mind Dorothy Parker, especially as she became famous for her brilliant short stories. She had a passionate friendship with D. H. Lawrence, who compared her to Dickens and later wrote that he used her as the model for Gudrun in *Women in Love.* Her biographer Antony Alpers was assisted by material freely given by both of her husbands and a close friend whom she called "wife," and by her two sisters, a cousin and two former lovers. Middleton Murry left Alpers entirely free to publish whatever he had determined that was true.

When she first arrived in the south of France in 1915, she was suffering from tuberculosis, and when she finally left in 1921, she was dying. What lay between these years were four flights from English winters, four futile pilgrimages to the sun. It was Menton that killed her. Menton with its still, enervating, pine-laden climate is fatal for consumptives. I have nowhere seen so many gravestones of the young—among them that of Aubrey Beardsley, dead at twenty-six—as in Menton's cemetery.

She had gone first to Bandol, a beach resort where some of the first tourists, Thomas Mann, Aldous Huxley, Marcel Pagnol, and Mistinguett, had stayed, but she found it too commercial, and so moved farther along the coast to Menton on the other side of Nice. John Middleton Murry came to visit her and they went for walks among the hills behind the town. However, he soon returned to London, leaving her to recuperate during the winter months.

She wrote every day, sometimes twice a day, to him and one wonders if he answered as frequently. She was bored, no doubt, even though she was beginning to fall in love with the beauty of the south of France, and she describes many of her days vividly as she went on numerous walks, missing him constantly. In one letter she wrote, "Ah, I wanted you today. Today I have longed for you. Have you known that? Can I long for you and you not know?"

December 20th

A lovely "gold dust" day. From early morning the fishermen have been passing and the little boats with red sails put out at dawn. When I woke this morning and opened the shutters and saw the dimpling sea I knew I was beginning to love this place—this south of France. Yesterday I went for a walk. The palm trees after the rain were magnificent, so firm and so green and standing up like stiff bouquets before the Lord.

Oh, Bogey, it is the most heavenly day. Every little tree feels it and waves faintly from delight. The femme de chambre called to the gardener just now as she beat the next door mattress out of the window—"Fait bon?" and he said "Ah, delicieux!" which seemed to me very funny for a gardener.

Her letters to Murry describe her infatuation with the scenery and her daily life in the south of France. Her poetry and her short stories were all about the region. At that time, she was not married to John, so she was looking forward to a wedding when she returned to England. Most of her letters to him were love letters, looking forward to the day when they would wed. She wrote to him:

I wish you could see the winds playing on the dark blue sea today . . . the clouds are like swans . . . the air tastes like fruit. Yesterday I went for a long scrambling walk in the woods, on the other side of the railway. There are no roads there, just a little track and old mule paths. Parts are quite wild and overgrown, then in all sorts of unexpected faery places you find a little clearing—the ground cultivated in tiny red terraces and sheltered by olive trees. There grow the jonquils, daffodils, new green peas and big abundant rose bushes, they are dream places. Every now and then I would hear a rustle in the bushes and an old, old, woman, her head tied up in a black kerchief, would come creeping through the thick tangle with a bunch of that pink heath across her shoulders. Once I found myself right at the very top of a hill and below there lay an immense valley—surrounded by mountains—very high ones—and it was so clear you could see every pointed pine, every little

> *zig-zag track—the black stems of the olives showing sooty and soft*
> *among the silvery green.*
>
> *Oh Bogey, how I longed for my playfellow! Why weren't you with me?*

And, another letter, written on Christmas Eve:

> *Yesterday after I had posted your letter I went to the Market. You know*
> *where that is, in front of that curious little Church. Yesterday the Market*
> *was full of roses, branches of mandarins and flowers of all kinds. There*
> *was also a little old man selling blue spectacles and rings "contre la rhu-*
> *matisme" and a funny fat old woman waddling about.*

When I went there on my passionate pilgrimage, I found that old market. I sat at a café and drank a café au lait, watching the locals buying and selling fruit and flowers, and then walked up to the villa, which is now privately owned and its shutters were closed. In the next-door garden, mounted on a very rickety chair, an old man in a blue apron and horn specs was snapping twigs, and below him a tiny little boy in pink and white socks received them in his apron.

In another letter to Murry she wrote, "Two of the big sailing ships have come right into the port this morning and are anchored close to the quai. I think they are unloading something." Her letters describe her joy at being there and her love affair with the area.

I too wanted to walk down those country lanes and the little paths she followed from the villa, and the valley she described. I found them all. The weather was glorious and there were daffodils everywhere and roses. How could one describe it all over again when she had done it so beautifully?

She also read a great deal, and said that to alleviate her insomnia and night fevers she would read Dickens, but that sometimes even he did not calm her. She writes:

> *I don't dare to work any more tonight. I suffer so frightfully from*
> *insomnia here and from night terrors. My work excites me so tremen-*
> *dously that I almost feel insane at night and I have been at it with hardly*
> *a break all day. But there is a great black bird flying over me, and I am*

so frightened he'll settle—so terrified I don't know exactly what kind he is. If I were not working here, with war and anxiety I should go mad, I think.

March 4th

Yesterday we went to La Turbie. It's up, up, high, high on the tops of the mountains. I could hardly bear it yesterday. I was so much in love with you. I kept seeing it all, for you—wishing for you—longing for you. The rosemary is in flower (our plant is). The almond trees, pink and white, there are wild cherry trees and prickly pear white among the olives. Apple trees are just in their first rose and white—wild hyacinths and violets are tumbled out of Flora's wicker ark and are everywhere. And over everything, like a light, are the lemon and orange trees glowing. If I saw one house which was ours, I saw twenty. I know we shall never live in such houses, but still they are ours—little houses with terraces and a verandah—with bean fields in bloom with a bright scatter of anemones all over the gardens. When we reached the mountain tops we got out and lay on the grass, looking down, down—into the valleys and over Monaco.

We stayed there about 2 hours and then dropped down by another road to Monte—the light and the shadow were divided on the hills, but the sun was still in the air, all the time—the sea was very rosy with a pale big moon over by Bordighera. We got home by 6.30 and there was my fire, the bed turned down—hot milk—May waiting to take off all my things. Did you enjoy it, Madam? Can you imagine such a coming to Life?

Menton is probably the quietest town on the French Riviera, known in the last century as a place where retired people came to die, especially the British. It is still very beautiful, away from the tourists of Cannes and Nice. The walks, the markets and the harbor that Katherine Mansfield describes are still almost untouched. It was a particular pleasure to discover this, as it was to read her short stories in the little café, just along the promenade where they had been written.

Paul Bowles

Chapter Nine

Paul Bowles in Morocco

Anybody who has seen the film *Casablanca* will remember Rick's Place with Humphrey Bogart as the proprietor. On seeing the movie again recently, I was surprised that I didn't remember how glamorous the place seemed to be. The clientele at Rick's are dressed in evening clothes, the men in tuxedos and Ingrid Bergman wears sexy dresses, a diamond pin, chic suits and lovely hats. The place was almost as chic as a New York nightclub like El Morocco. There was not only Sam the pianist playing but, in some of the scenes, a small orchestra. I had remembered the place more as a bistro, but look again at how exotic the people and Rick's Place were in that film! Casablanca and Tangier were faraway places with strange sounding names that gave the impression of not only being dangerous, but exotic and sensual. I yearned to go and see it all, even though I'd heard that young girls could be kidnapped and whisked away for the "white slave traffic." How different from our life back home! It all seemed to be so glamorous, so colorful, with different kinds of strange foods. Couscous, lamb dishes, paella, baked fish.

You read of the murders in the Casbah and the drug trade, of course. Writers and artists who went to live in Morocco often slid into debauchery and wicked ways. You only have to remember what happened to Sebastian in Evelyn Waugh's *Brideshead Revisited,* or the couple in Bowles's novel, *The Sheltering Sky.*

But then there were the lovely beaches, the tropical warm air, the perfume of the exotic flowers, and the wonderful spices and herbs. Arriving in Morocco is a little like arriving in France years ago, the aroma of the Gauloise cigarettes, cigars, strong coffee and garlic permeating everywhere. Like Paris, Tangier doesn't really have those perfumes or smells anymore. I went to live in Tangier for six months to discover what living there would be like, and to experience the climate in which writers such as Paul and Jane Bowles and David Herbert lived in the 1950s. Because of the heat, they lived in Moorish houses, decorated with colorful tiles, pottery, fountains and palm trees. They had no need for heavy clothes or winter home furnishings, and they avoided the trouble of commuting in traffic, as in London or New York.

Tangier was a small city where you could walk almost anywhere, with colorful markets on every street—fruits, vegetables, meat, jewelry, materials, carpets—in an Arabian nights setting with Moroccan sellers plying their trade. In the Casbah it was a similar setting. But it wasn't a good idea to walk alone after sundown, though much of the nightlife was centered there. Down by the waterfront, there were restaurants and bars, which were off the tourist track when I was there. For the locals, there were floor shows, always featuring Flamenco dancers, with one or two guitarists playing for them. I am sure today there are far more of these places, now geared to the cruise ship passengers and tourists.

It felt very foreign to be there. The French quarter had luxury shops, selling French perfume and cosmetics, beautiful objets d'art and fashions directly from Paris. Back in the hills behind Tangier were huge mansions of the very rich, so you knew that there were plenty of clients for these fashions. The main streets were very sleek, similar to the Croisette in Cannes, and there was the feel of the Riviera in parts of the coastline. Perhaps I wanted to feel the excitement of those film characters, each one depending on Rick getting them an exit visa. It is amusing, though, to see what wardrobes they all had. Who, nowadays, in a desperate situation would put on a tuxedo or dinner jacket, white no less, to go and drink martinis and dine at Rick's? It is amusing to see the customers at Rick's acting like Fred Astaire and Ginger Rogers, about to get up and dance as they watch the Germans descend on the café.

While in Morocco I lived rather like that actually. I became a nanny for the American political attaché and his wife, who entertained a great deal. We would have sumptuous dinners of Moroccan food, and afterward flamenco dancers and guitarists would entertain us in the marble reception room overlooking the Mediterranean. The babysitting was easy: just a quick look every so often upstairs. I had a wonderful time, meeting American, French, British diplomats at dinner, then some free time in the early evenings, when the family would spend time at home with the child. Free to do or go where I liked, I decided to try to find a job.

A British businessman whom I had met on the ferry coming over from Gibraltar invited me for a drink at the chic Velasquez Hotel. I was bowled over by the place. A glassed-in cocktail bar on the roof offered a view of all Tangier. Everything was white, mirrors reflected the view over the city, and the glasses lined up behind the bar matched the glass of the windows. There was a white grand piano with a large flower arrangement on top. Fred Astaire and Ginger Rogers could have walked in at any moment.

Tangier

The barman asked me to play something, as I had walked over to look at the piano. So I did. As it happened, the owner of the hotel was having a drink at the bar, and later on he offered me a job as a pianist for the afternoon crowd from four to five-thirty, four days a week. I had found a job! And somewhere to practice the piano, of course.

I had also gone to see if I could find the American writer Paul Bowles who I knew lived there with his wife, Jane. Little did I know he was spending that year in California. But I still wanted to stay in Tangier, and so kept my job and then found a new one at the American School. I discovered years later that Paul Bowles had composed the music for several productions that the American School had presented. Well, I shrugged, at least I had worked there for a time.

When Bowles had been in Paris, he knew many of the American writers there, and it was Gertrude Stein who suggested he visit Tangier and Morocco. So his first visit to Tangier was with his friend and music teacher, the composer Aaron Copland. Bowles then went to Berlin and met the writer Christopher Isherwood (who gives the name Bowles to the heroine of *Goodbye to Berlin*). The following year he returned to North Africa and decided to settle in Tangier. His music was more prominent than his work as a writer and he composed a great deal. For the next ten years he composed a great volume of work, including the music for the film *Doctor Faustus,* directed by Orson Welles, and also the orchestration for George Balanchine's "Yankee Clipper."

He married Jane Auer, an author and playwright, and after a brief sojourn in France they were prominent among the literary figures of New York throughout the 1940s. His light opera, *The Wind Remains,* based on a poem by Garcia Lorca, was performed in 1943, with choreography by Merce Cunningham and conducted by Leonard Bernstein. Then in 1943 he began to write fiction, beginning with short stories. But in 1947 he went to live in Tangier and his wife, Jane, followed him there shortly afterward. They quickly became part of the group of expatriates in Tangier. Many of their literary friends came to visit, including Gore Vidal, Truman Capote, Tennessee Williams, Allen Ginsberg and many British writers, too. David Herbert, the son of the Earl of Pembroke, who lived in the family mansion at Wilton in Salisbury, had settled in Tangier, much to the disappointment of his aristocratic father. The Herberts had an illustrious history going back to Shakespeare's time, when some historians say that the real Dark Lady of the Sonnets was the then–Lady Pembroke, the object of the Bard's affections. Noël Coward and Somerset Maugham visited him, too, and Tangier became the "Paris of the South." Writers, artists and wealthy patrons like Barbara Hutton had homes there. The combination of the exotic locale, the warmer weather and the European zones in Tangier made it a very colorful and sophisticated place to live, for expats from all parts of Europe.

I wanted to be part of this scene, especially in midwinter. I took a ship from London to Gibraltar, and from there across to Morocco on the ferry, the same ferry that was featured in the Alec Guinness movie, *A Captain's Paradise,* when he, as the Captain, had a woman both in Gibraltar and Tangier. The people I met when I was working at the American School, or playing cocktail piano in the rooftop bar at the Hotel Velasquez, were characters that could have been from a novel. Some of them became famous and some infamous. I met a group of smugglers, for example. There was a bar called The Leopard Room, where most Brits gathered each evening. One night I was there with friends, when a group of Brits came in and sat beside us. They were all very jolly, but no one had seen them before, so we knew they were newcomers. I talked to a young girl who was obviously with the leader of the group, since we happened to go to the wash room at the same time. She seemed rather sweet, too young to be in the bar really, but then who asked in those days? I asked what they were doing in Tangier, and she replied they had just arrived on Bill's large yacht. When I asked what they were doing here, she said they had a delivery of gin from Spain. The boys had been busy renaming the gin. When I seemed confused she offered, "Oh, they just change the labels." She obviously didn't think there was anything wrong about this. I smiled to myself. They were bringing in rot-gut gin from Spain and relabeling it with some well-known label and selling it as such. I decided not to get involved and left the bar shortly afterward. A few days later I met a couple who were planning to open an expensive weight-loss clinic—and feed the customers water pills, in the guise of a wonder drug. So the city was full of adventurers and crooks, as well as writers and poets.

During this period I was trying to write. Long letters home and to my friends described the city, my work and the people I was meeting—I'd nearly convinced myself to settle there. However, this pilgrimage was proving more exotic than I first imagined and Tangier was really lovely in those days. Just a few years later, Morocco reclaimed the city, so it was no longer an international zone and all the European businesses and residents left. However, when I was there, the French and Spanish quarters, the Moroccans and British coexisted side by side. There was a British church and an American School, with many interracial events which were fascinating because of the mixture of cultures. I would have stayed longer, but I had met and fallen in love with the ship's doctor on the ship back from Australia after touring there with the Old Vic Company. He was about to leave for postgraduate work in the States and wanted me to go with him. By that time, Paul Bowles had bought an island off the coast of Ceylon in India and had moved there. However, he did return to Tangier, where he died of heart failure in 1999 at the age of eighty-eight. Although he had lived in Tangier for over fifty years, he was buried in Lakemont, New York, next to the graves of his parents and grandparents. He had published fourteen short story collections, numerous volumes of poetry, travel articles, and an autobiography. He was also a music ethnologist, deeply interested in Moroccan traditional music and, when he was in his mid-fifties, was close to the Master Musicians of Jajouka. His novels were bestsellers, including, of course, *The Sheltering Sky.*

Jane Bowles was a fascinating woman and a brilliant author in her own right. An accomplished linguist, she spoke French, Spanish and Arabic, all self-taught. From 1947 she had been traveling and living in all parts of the world, from Paris to Ceylon. She wandered all over Europe, then from there went to Central America and Mexico, before going to Tangier, with Paul. She published a highly regarded novel titled *Two Serious Ladies,* and at one time was a tenant, together with her husband in a boardinghouse in Brooklyn Heights run by George Davis. Some of the other tenants included W. H. Auden, Benjamin Britten, Carson McCullers and Oliver Smith. When she and her husband settled in Tangier they became permanent Tangerinos, inviting friends to come and stay. Like Paul, she wrote many short stories. The couple was able to write in Tangier as well as entertain most of the people they had left behind in Paris and New York. Truman Capote recalled that his most satisfying memories of Jane revolved around a month spent in side-by-side rooms in a pleasantly shabby hotel on the rue du Bac in Paris during the icy winter of January 1951. They spent long evenings in Jane's snug room ("fat with books and papers and foodstuffs and a snappy white Pekinese puppy bought from a Spanish sailor, long evenings spent listening to a phonograph and drinking warm applejack while Jane built sloppy, marvelous stews atop an electric burner"). She was a good cook and cooking was one of her extracurricular gifts.

Truman also writes of her spooky ability to mimic certain singers, such as Helen Morgan and Libby Holman. He wrote a story years later, called "Among the Paths of Eden," in which he described several of Jane's characteristics without realizing it: her stiff-legged limp, her spectacles, and her brilliant and poignant abilities as a mimic.

She also wrote a play called *In the Summer House,* which was produced in New York, and Capote, who said he found it difficult to sit through any play, went to see it three times, he enjoyed it so much. When discussing the difficulty of writing, she spoke of a mutual friend, another writer, saying "But it is so easy for him. He only has to turn his hand. Just turn his hand." Capote adds that actually writing is never easy, in case anyone doesn't know. It's the hardest work around, he thought, and for Jane it was difficult to the point of pain.

Capote said that he thought Jane's "Camp Cataract" was her most complete story, and most representative of her work. In his introduction to the volume of her short stories, he writes: "It is a rending sample of controlled compassion: a comic tale of doom that has at its heart and as its heart, the subtlest comprehension of eccentricity and human apartness." Jane died and was buried in 1973 in Malaga, Spain. Paul decided to continue living in Tangier. He narrated the Bertolucci film adaptation of his novel, *The Sheltering Sky,* ending the film with these words.

> Because we don't know when we will die we get to think of life as an inexhaustible well. Yet, everything happens only a certain number of times, and a very small number really. How many times will you remember a certain afternoon of your childhood? Perhaps four or five times more, perhaps not even that. How many more times will you watch the new moon rise, perhaps twenty and yet it all seems limitless.

Cole Porter

Chapter Ten

Cole Porter in Paris

Whenever I had a weekend to spare from working in London I would go to Paris to visit all the places I had read about as a student. First, I visited every address where George Sand had lived alone and then later with Chopin. Next, I went to all the venues where Chopin had played as well as his apartment in the Place Vendome, where he died. Those essential first outings accomplished, however, I moved on to the more modern musicians who had lived in Paris, particularly the Americans such as Cole Porter, one of my favorites.

Cole and Linda Porter bought a house at 13 Rue Monsieur and spent a great deal of time there between 1920 and 1937. The house was featured in a 1925 edition of *Vogue* magazine, with photos showing a circular entrance, a floor of black and white marble and a white marble staircase leading to the bedrooms above. The main reception room was filled with red Chinese lacquered tables, statues, art deco furnishings, cream taffeta drapes and zebra rugs, as well as a full-sized Steinway piano, which is now in the Episcopal Church in Paris. A hardwood floor was installed in the basement, transforming it into a ballroom. The walls were lined with mirrors and banquettes, and a bandstand was erected as well.

Both Robert Kimball and William McBrien wrote about the life of Cole Porter; the list of celebrities who danced and partied at his Paris home is a who's who of society between the wars: Elsa Maxwell, Fred and Adele Astaire, Howard Sturges, Diana Vreeland, the Duke and Duchess of Windsor, Elsie de Wolfe, Noël Coward, Nancy Mitford, Duff and Lady Diana Cooper and Jimmy Donahue. The American performer Bricktop went to the house to teach Cole and his friends to dance the

Charleston. F. Scott Fitzgerald insisted: "My greatest claim to fame is that I discovered Bricktop before Cole Porter did."

Here is Michael Arlen's caricature of Porter: "Every morning at half past seven Cole Porter leaps lightly out of bed and, having said his prayers, arranges himself in riding habit. Then having written a song or two, he will appear at the stroke of half past twelve at the Ritz, where leaning in a manly way on the bar, he will say, 'Champagne cocktail, please. Had a marvelous ride this morning!' "

Ah, the Ritz, that famous bar central to so much literary and artistic life. The Ritz Bar, well described in Fitzgerald's *Babylon Revisited,* was where he and Hemingway used to meet almost every day. Cole Porter was also a regular, as were Coco Chanel, Bernard Berenson, Cecil Beaton, Jack Buchanan, Sir Charles and Lady Mendl, and Gerald and Sara Murphy. A friend of the Murphys wrote of a meeting he had with Cole in the Ritz bar: "He introduced me to the Duke of Alba who was costumed as

Steve Ross, performing at the Ritz Hotel, Paris

a chorus man and trailing a dog named Snookums on a silver chain. A very odd scene."

Cole Porter first met the woman who would become his wife at the Ritz, Linda Lee Thomas. They both were attending the wedding of Ethel Harriman and Henry Russell in 1918. Cole and Linda were married on December 12 of the following year in the Town Hall in the Eighth Arrondissement, and began their life of travel, parties and mixing with the crème de la crème in the south of France, Venice and around the world. From childhood, Cole was uncommonly curious and loved to travel. Linda was keen on travel as well.

Moss Hart, who also visited their Paris home, commented: "Their house in Paris was exquisite, one of the most beautiful houses I have ever seen, and Linda Porter, a legendary beauty herself, lent something of her own radiance and splendor." The story goes that Moss Hart first met Cole Porter in Paris on a trip in 1932, armed with a letter of introduction from Irving Berlin. Two years later, as their friendship developed, they decided to spend time together writing a new musical. Hart wanted to spend the winter months in Morocco, but Cole thought that the South Seas would be better, so in the end they decided to go around the world on the luxurious Cunard ship, the *Franconia*. They left on January 12, 1935, and when they arrived back they had written a musical called *Jubilee*.

Visiting the Ritz Bar years later, in 2006, I found it deserted and spied a beautiful grand piano in the hallway, which was not being used. I thought, wouldn't it be great to be able to present a cabaret featuring the music of Cole Porter and Noël Coward in the very place they loved so much? In September 2006, I wrote to the owner of the Ritz Hotel to ask if I might present an American-style cabaret similar to the shows at the Algonquin or Carlyle Hotels in New York. I loved listening to Bobby Short, Elaine Stritch and Eartha Kitt in New York, and I wanted to replicate that atmosphere in Paris. I was delighted to be given permission to do so, and the venue was the Ritz's Bar Vendome, which has seats for more people than the smaller, though more famous bar. So, one of my latest pilgrimages was to recapture some of the spirit and joie de vivre of those times. Whereas the small bar was world renowned for the writers it attracted, I had an idea to bring back the cabaret of Cole Porter, a sort of tribute to these brilliant American composers whose haunt was the Ritz bar—something like the cabarets that

Elizabeth Sharland and Steve Ross

the Porters use to organize in their home or when they went to Venice. They invited the black singer/pianist Leslie Hutchinson, known as "Hutch," to stay with them in Venice, as he was the popular artist who played at Quaglino's in London and was the rage in Europe.

I contacted Steve Ross, the king of cabaret in America, and asked him if he would come over and play at the Ritz. He happened to be in Europe at the time, so he was available and we set a date in October 2006. I was delighted to be able to promote the first American cabaret at the Ritz for many years. It was a privilege to introduce Steve to a packed room, where he proceeded to charm the whole crowd, including the waiters who stopped to listen. If it hadn't been for the full cooperation of the staff at the Ritz as well as Mr. Mohammed Al Fayed, it would never have happened. The reunion of such great composers, with such great songs, with such a great interpreter as Steve Ross made the pilgrimage well worth it.

New pilgrimages come about as time goes by, and those places you desired to visit change. What you wanted to see in your teenage years are not the same forty years later. People who have never visited Paris, Venice or the other great cities of Europe are maybe interested in seeing the museums and the Old Masters, but after having seen these, I have found it more fulfilling to wander in the gardens of homes, or visit the smaller towns where people like Puccini, Verdi and Sand lived and worked. My parents used to read H. V. Morton's books, which were very popular travel guides. His *In Search of* . . . books sold extremely well.

View from home of Victor Hugo, Place des Vosges

Chapter Eleven

Victor Hugo in Paris

The home of Victor Hugo is at No. 9 Place des Vosges, one of the oldest squares in Paris. Cardinal Richelieu, who lived at No. 21, later had a bronze statue of Louis XIII erected in the center of the square. Today, the Place des Vosges is a calm oasis in bustling Paris. Through the stone archways, under the first floor of the buildings are coffee shops, boutiques and heavily trafficked streets. But inside the small garden in the center of the square, one can walk in peace among hedges, flowers and the especially wonderful trees. Even in years past, the Place des Vosges must have been a sanctuary from all the nearby activity. The streets of the Marais, Paris's oldest district, teemed with stores and people, and the Bastille was nearby.

Victor Hugo was born in 1802 and his fame came early. His first collection of poetry was published when he was just twenty-one years old, and for it he won a royal pension from Louis XVIII. He published another collection of poetry two years later and his writing career was established. He fell in love with Adèle Foucher but they didn't marry until 1821, after his mother's death, because she did not approve of his choice. Their first child died in infancy, but then they had two sons and a daughter. He published his first full-length novel, *The Hunchback of Notre Dame,* in 1831, and between 1829 and 1840 he would write five more volumes of poetry.

But his political writings got him into trouble. One of his most controversial political plays (all his plays were political), *Hernani,* caused riots when it was produced in Paris because it was interpreted as an attack on the aristocracy. (In a precursor of the later adaptation of Hugo's work into a musical form, *Hernani* was later turned into an opera by Verdi.) But his real trouble began when he penned *The Little Napoleon,*

99

criticizing the dictator for overthrowing the democracy, such as it was, and then *The History of a Crime*, saying that Napoleon had usurped his power and was a traitor to France. Hugo was forced to go into exile.

He first went to Brussels, then to Jersey and finally to Guernsey in the Channel Islands, where he stayed for twenty years. His house is now a museum open to the public. It was there, in Hauteville House, that he wrote several novels, including *Les Misérables*. When he finally was allowed to return to Paris in 1870, things did not go well for him. He suffered a small stroke and his daughter had to be committed to an insane asylum. His two sons had died, and he lost his wife in 1876. Juliette Drouet, his mistress of over thirty years, also died. But he continued his political life and was very popular with the masses. He was elected to the legislature, mainly because of his writings and his sympathy for the plight of the workers and the poor. He was declared a national hero, had a state funeral which over two million attended, and was buried in the Pantheon.

The quantity of his poetry, novels and plays is astonishing. People remarked after meeting Hugo about the energy of the man, and how both he and his work were forces of nature. The story of how he managed to coordinate the life of a politician, a father, a novelist, a poet and a host on every Sunday to dozens of writers, playwrights and performers would take another book. Many have been written, of course, and it is worthwhile to read one before going to visit his home.

I found the Place des Vosges and his home at No 9. The museum is open most days and admission is free. The old polished parquet floor in the entrance way is original, and as you ascend the very wide wood staircase, it is as if you have stepped back into the 1880s. The rooms are all on one floor upstairs, and as you pass through them you can sense how it must have been when Hugo lived, wrote and entertained here. Large windows let light into the main salon, where Hugo invited all the great thinkers of the day to discuss politics, the latest novel or the human condition. He was at the center of a Parisian creative colony of politicians, lawyers, civic figures, writers, painters, journalists and musicians, including Liszt, George Sand, Alfred de Musset, Balzac, Flaubert, Lamartine, Turgenev and Delacroix. Hugo was a painter himself, and Delacroix remarked that if Hugo had not been a writer, he could have outshone the famous artists of that century. Much of his work has been carefully stored in the floor above at No 9, where it can be still seen.

But when you visit his home, you might think, if you weren't told whose house it was, that it had belonged to an art collector or bank president. Hugo transformed it into a unique and elegant space full of exotic paintings, furniture and collections of china, crystal and rugs, which can be seen today. There are over a hundred decorative plates lining the walls of his reception room, which has an Oriental motif throughout. It is one of the most astonishing rooms I have seen in all my travels.

Hugo was a defender of the common man, yet enjoyed considerable wealth. He paid the price of exile and great personal loss, but gave much of his life over to improving the lot of his fellow Frenchmen. He could have taken the gains of his prolific writing and left for the Riviera or elsewhere, but he stayed in Paris and worked up until the very end. He was still writing when he died at the age of eighty-six, in 1888. As many artists do, he surrounded himself with other artists and their works. He filled his salon with debate and music and covered his walls with works of beauty. Other than Dickens with London, there are few artists as associated with a city as Hugo is with Paris, and you should see his home in order to understand the city as well as Hugo's mind and his time.

Franco Zeffirelli

Chapter Twelve

Franco Zeffirelli in Positano, Italy

Elizabeth Taylor, Richard Burton, Mel Gibson, Judi Dench, Glenn Close, Maggie Smith, Leonard Bernstein and famous European performers from France, Italy and Germany have all worked for Zeffirelli. Maria Callas, Joan Sutherland, Luciano Pavarotti, Placido Domingo and many others have sung for him. Actors, singers, composers and producers who have worked with him sing his praises.

Zeffirelli is one of the towering figures of modern theatre, a man whose career has spanned four decades and brought him to the heights of his profession as director of both operas and movies. His opera productions command sellout performances on both sides of the Atlantic.

Many people agree that opera lovers are a breed apart. You are either exposed to this genre as a child and grow up with the music, just as some families play classical music rather than popular songs, or a chance encounter occurs one day, later in your life. For thousands of people, that chance encounter came when they saw and heard the Three Tenors. For some, it was the first time they had ever heard an aria from an opera.

The thrill of a great artist singing is universal. I had been following the career of Dame Joan Sutherland ever since she left the shores of Australia. Pavarotti called her voice "the voice of the century," and her many recordings are still available, even though she retired in 1990. Almost the same number of people who listened to the Three Tenors began to love opera after seeing Franco Zeffirelli's feature film of *La Traviata,* starring Placido Domingo. The film captured not only the brilliant music, lyrics and pathos of the opera, but also the visual beauty of the Parisian settings, the costumes, the décor, including the Paris town house, the furnishings, the chandeliers and the society of a bygone age. Of course, his films are seen best in widescreen with Dolby sound rather than on video, where so much of the impact is lost.

When Zeffirelli first listened to Dame Joan sing, he knew in thirty seconds that she would become a great star. The two of them began their careers in opera at almost the same time, with Sutherland singing and Zeffirelli directing. He had worked equally successfully with Callas, so it must have been difficult for him to work with both of them at that time, because of differences in their temperaments.

Norman Ayrton was Joan's dramatic and acting coach, who also taught her how to move on stage and learn how to fall properly, because some of the great divas either have to "die," or at least faint, on stage. Ayrton also explained how they had to work on her "general pained expression," or what they dubbed it her "G.P.E.," when singing dramatic roles.

Zeffirelli has been constantly criticized for his lavish and expensive productions. However, they are still presented in the world's top theatres, including the Metropolitan in New York, and at the Royal Opera House in London. The argument against him is that he overspends his budget by having too many actors and singers on stage, with extremely expensive sets. But he makes the scenes look alive; the choirs, the parades, the street crowds are all part of the spectacle. He fills the empty spaces with color and action, puts raw passion on stage to go with the music, and visually sweeps you away with the beauty of his staging.

Born in Florence in 1923, in his autobiography he reveals a shocking childhood that is partially presented in his feature film, *Tea with Mussolini*, starring Maggie Smith, Judi Dench, Cher and Lily Tomlin as well as Lady Olivier (Joan Plowright). The day he had to stand up in class and reveal he was the only illegitimate boy in the classroom was a humiliation he still remembers.

Later he was an apprentice to the legendary Italian director of opera, films and theatre Luchino Visconti. Visconti was a generous mentor and taught him to direct, to design both costumes and sets, as well as the production. Visconti was part of the Italian aristocracy, the intelligentsia, who experienced the elegance, sophistication and the cosmopolitan way of life in a world of professional artists, singers, composers and writers. Unfortunately we cannot see any of Visconti's opera productions, but some of his films are still available. He was a passionate man who recognized the same in Zeffirelli. This is the passion to inspire, teach—to translate all that opera has to give.

In the documentary that Zeffirelli made about the staging and sets for his production of *Tosca*, he explains on camera how he chose to replicate the actual settings where each of the three acts takes place. He also tells why Act Two is almost like a bullfight, when Tosca suddenly turns and stabs Scarpia, who is about to seduce her. It is one of the most dramatically charged acts in any opera.

I wondered what the interiors of their various homes would be like. I knew that Visconti had a sumptuous villa on Lake Como, while Zeffirelli had an exquisite apartment in Rome.

In his autobiography, Zeffirelli recalls visiting two friends, who invited him to stay at the Villa Treville years earlier, Bob Ullman and Donald Downes, who owned the villa then. When Franco needed a bolt hole to escape from Rome, he went to stay with them in Positano. He writes:

> They really were "the odd couple." Although never anything but friends, theirs was a sort of marriage. They bickered the whole time and quarreled about everything from food to the books with which the villa was piled high. But if anyone else dared to criticize the one to the other, then let the third party beware.

Positano

105

When Bob was killed in a car accident, Donald didn't want to stay on and offered the villa to Zeffirelli. The contents were all put up for auction, but Zeffirelli bought them back. After Donald's death in California he brought Donald's ashes back to Italy to be buried in the garden. Earlier, when Zeffirelli first took over the villa, he transformed it and told Donald that he wanted to create his own dream world, which he did. The villa is actually three little villas on separate levels. He named one Romeo, another Juliet, and the third Mercutio. He loved decorating and creating theatre, so he started renovations.

> Each place had a different character: I kept the eighteenth- and nineteenth-century Neapolitan style of the upper villa; the red house that Diaghilev had used I also kept in period; while I lavished all my theatricality on the large white space full of mirrors and palms, and all around terraces and verandahs, stepped gardens and little secret walkways with hanging plants, flower beds and exotic shrubs.

He kept adding to it, a grotto, a new bathing place, a vegetable garden, a games court. There are about three thousand plants, some of them very rare, which had been planted by Donald. A year after the renovations Donald went to visit Zeffirelli, who was very nervous, waiting that day for his friend's arrival.

> However, I needn't have worried. He was in a mood of cynical good humour, and after looking at the white salon he said: "Oh, yes, very beautiful, but when can we see the second act?" He then added that it looked a bit like the new Holiday Inn, Tunis, "but it could have been a lot worse—a Casablanca Hilton."

The following summer, my husband and I had planned a vacation in Capri and Positano. Curiously, the week before departure I read a magazine article about the Villa Treville, just outside Positano. The photos looked sensational and it seemed a coincidence that we were going to Positano the following week. The town is on the Amalfi Coast, with old terraced houses, in every color, layered down to the sea. Tiny alleyways with dozens of steps and archways form the central part of the tiny town.

Cars cannot descend all the way down, so if your hotel is near the beach, you end up walking to it.

I had dedicated my book, *A Theatrical Feast,* to Zeffirelli, so I took a copy with me in case we would see him there. But after a few days, and not having his phone number, we decided to walk to his villa one morning and leave it in his mailbox, as our hotel proprietor knew he wasn't in residence that week.

However, we couldn't find the mailbox and his house seemed to be down a very long flight of stone steps going toward the beach. We walked down until we came to a wrought-iron gate on one side, behind which was a little barking dog, which I recognized was Zeffirelli's, as I had seen the photo of them together in the article.

A young woman appeared and we explained we had come to leave the book. The dog stopped barking as she opened the gate and invited us in, and we gave her the book. We spoke Italian well enough to tell her I had dedicated the book to Zeffirelli

Zeffirelli's garden at Positano

and that I had met him in New York several months previously. At that time, we had had a forty-five-minute conversation about cremation, of all things, and he told me about the quickness of Callas's cremation without her friends even knowing about it.

The villa was just as I imagined it to be: there was a beautiful reception room with white sofas and white rugs, crystal, china, antique furniture, a wall full of decorative vases, a statue of the Madonna on the coffee table and rare exotic draperies.

The actual location and setting is very dramatic, as the house is on a high cliff that looks out on to higher cliffs in the distance, all of which descend into the Mediterranean Sea, beyond the small bay below. As I sat on the patio, I thought of all the fabulous parties that had been held on this spot. Opera stars, theatre people, like the Oliviers, who often stayed there, all ate and drank out here, admiring the view, maybe with a few impromptu arias thrown in, and much laughter. I looked out at the view again and realized it is very similar to the view that Noël Coward had when he was living on the south coast of England—his home there looked out onto one of the high cliffs of Dover.

Later on, saying goodbye to our host, we continued walking down the stone steps, along a sandy track, through a passage at the bottom of the path which led on to a sandy beach. From there you could look up and see the balustrade of the villa's patio high above.

Many years later I met Zeffirelli again in New York, when he was attending the premiere of his film, *Callas Forever,* starring Fanny Ardent and Jeremy Irons. It was Franco's tribute to Callas. After Onassis had married Jacqueline Kennedy she became a recluse, and then became ill and was taking all kinds of pills, mainly sleeping pills. She refused to see any of her friends, but Zeffirelli says he still feels very guilty and that he should have insisted and forced his way into see and comfort her. This film is a fantasy about just that, a fictional story about what happens when he does make his way into her home and tries to comfort her with more work.

It is astonishing that his genius doesn't seem to be recognized in New York as much as it should be, mainly because of the budget he requires, but also due to a strange kind of uneasiness at his brilliance. He wrote a letter to the *New York Times* several years ago, saying how bitter criticism can destroy an artist so totally that they can't create anymore. He cited a classical composer, who, after a stinging review, wrote no more music for twenty years. Let these same critics try their hands at set and costumes design, directing a cast of opera singers, inspiring thousands of patrons with new and innovative ideas!

Elizabeth Sharland with Zeffirelli

His being from Italy, indeed from Florence—with a mentor like Visconti, with his successes at La Fenice in Venice and all the great opera houses in Europe—should give a clear indication of his authority and deep understanding of the creative world.

During that same week, we crossed over to the island of Capri to follow in the footsteps of Graham Greene. I was armed with Shirley Hazzard's book *Graham Greene on Capri*. It proved a very useful guide and again it was a pleasure to see the same vistas, and the beauty of the flowers, pathways with flowery vines, rockeries with perfumed bushes, and blinding sunshine everywhere. I based part of my first novel on Capri.

Lady Gregory

Chapter Thirteen

Lady Gregory in County Galway

One of Ireland's most famous women has to be Lady Gregory, who together with W. B. Yeats founded the legendary Abbey Theatre in Dublin, which is still running today.

She wrote over forty plays, many of which were first produced at the Abbey, until someone contended that the Abbey was losing its audience because of her plays. She also acted in several of them. When Synge's *Playboy of the Western World* was first produced there, it caused a riot and people threw things onto the stage and tried to stop the show. She said that "There is always the same dilemma between the Irish; there are those who use a toothbrush, and those who don't."

She was born in 1880 to an Anglo-Irish family named Persse in County Galway. Her mother was a strict evangelical Protestant and so she was brought up in a rigid household. There were no books or any kind of library. She married a much-traveled man, and even though he was thirty-five years older, they were happy together. They traveled widely, and after he died she settled in their country home called Coole Park, in County Galway. It was at this time she started writing. First she edited her husband's autobiography, writing, "If I had not married I should not have learned the quick enrichment of sentences that one gets in conversation: had I not been widowed I should not have found the detachment of mind, the leisure for observation necessary to give insight into character, to express and interpret it." She enjoyed the process so much she began writing her own work.

While she was living at Coole Park, she met W. B. Yeats who was staying at her neighbor Edward Martyn's house. The three of them had long conversations about Irish writers and founded the Irish Literary Theatre in 1899. During this time, she read and co-authored some of Yeats's early plays. A few years later this theatre folded due to lack of funds, but in 1904 they formed the Irish National Theatre with the financial aid of Anne Horniman, Synge, Yeats and several others. Horniman and William Fay bought the Hibernian Theatre in Lower Abbey Street and the adjoining building which was in Marlborough Street. Annie Horniman was not a resident of Ireland so the Government required that she hand it over to a resident, and that was Lady Gregory. On the opening night, December 27, 1904, one of Lady Gregory's plays, *Spreading the News,* opened the theatre.

She remained an active director of the Abbey until ill health led her to retirement in 1928. During this period, Coole Park was the ideal environment for playwrights and writers to work. On a tree in what were the grounds of the now-demolished house, one can still see the carved initials of Synge, AE, W. B. Yeats and his artist brother Jack, Sean O'Casey, George Bernard Shaw, Katherine Tynan and Violet Martin. Yeats wrote five poems about or set in the house and grounds: "The Wild Swans at Coole," "I walked among the seven woods of Coole," "In the Seven Woods," "Coole Park, 1929" and "Coole Park and Ballylee, 1931."

When I was taken to Dublin on my honeymoon by my Dublin-born husband, I was eager to go to the Abbey Theatre and to see all the old haunts of Lady Gregory and Yeats. Their period of literary history was called "the Celtic Twilight," but because my husband was a psychiatrist and knew the history of what these people wrote about, including Yeats and Maud Gonne, instead of the Celtic Twilight he nicknamed them "the Celtic Madhouse." So many of them were into spiritualism and the paranormal, and the Golden Dawn Society that George Bernard Shaw's mother was part of. The Georgian squares and the architecture of the city are wonderful and the pleasure of discovering where Yeats, Oscar Wilde and many others lived was very interesting. But it was Lady Gregory who brought the Celtic Twilight into being, which in turn partly inspired my own passionate pilgrimage to Dublin.

So, having been a passionate traveler since my earliest travels with my father in Tasmania, and then to the homes and shrines of the major literary and musical icons of Europe who achieved heroic status in my mind and heart, starting with my arrival in London, I am in a very real sense, a pilgrim and a most passionate one; thus this book is an honest account of my own Passionate Pilgrimages.

Postscript

Just as I was finishing this book, a few weeks ago, I came across the Web site of Woodbridge quite unexpectedly, and was astonished to see that my family's ancestral home in Tasmania had become a luxury hotel, winning an award as one of the small luxury hotels of the world. There was an article in the *New York Times* recently about Tasmania calling it a "Boutique-style Island." The once isolated and wild land has finally been discovered by the jet set.

My great-grandfather's home Woodbridge in New Norfolk, a picturesque town on the Derwent River just north of Hobart, was crumbling into ruin when I left the island. So, it was a pleasant surprise to discover that it had been restored to its original glory. It is situated on one of the most beautiful parts of the river, where the current is slow and most days the water is like a mirror reflecting the willow trees that line the river banks, reminiscent of the Loire Valley with its wonderful river reflections. My great-grandfather had been appointed the Surveyor-general of Tasmania, and there are geographic features including a mountain named after him. My own unusually good sense of direction is probably inherited from him.

Now the island grows its own wine, and Tasmanian Cascade beer has been famous for a century as one of the best in Australia. The fruit, the lamb, the seafood make it a very enjoyable place to visit. When I look back at the camping and picnics we used to have in the bush and then view the luxury hotels which are now being installed in the ancient homes, it is almost unbelievable to think of the changes in one lifetime.

My father, Michael Sharland, had a passion for preserving the earliest late Georgian structures in Tasmania, built mostly from gold-colored sandstone. He wrote a book called *Stones of a Century,* and we traveled up and down the country as he photographed and wrote about the wonderful old homes, bridges and buildings. He also photographed Woodbridge, when it was almost derelict, so he would have been very pleased to know that it has been saved.

He wrote: "These old structures make a strong appeal to our aesthetic sense and possess a peculiar charm. Many are entwined with history and serve to embellish and add to the beauty of our natural scenery, giving that grace which only historical association can give. I have attempted to preserve in pictures what will not be preserved by time and disuse. Many of the buildings are crumbling through inadequate care, many will soon be masses of rubble. Some have been converted into flats and guest houses; others are occupied by shepherds or stockmen quite unable to stay the decay and deterioration that goes on around them, so the houses crack and crumble, as soon there is a ruin where once a noble house stood."

My family home, Woodbridge, in Tasmania

Later on, as Superintendent of the Tasmanian Scenery Preservation Board, which is similar to the National Trust in Britain, he was put in charge of restoring one of these old homes, "Entally," filling it with period furniture and opening it to the public. It has become one of the top tourist attractions on the island.

So those journeys with his camera were his passionate pilgrimages. Maybe someone will make their own pilgrimage to Tasmania to see such a scenic and beautiful place.

www.sharland.com

Index

INDEX